Music in America

MUSIC IN AMERICA
USIC IN AMERICA M
ERICA MUSIC IN AM
MUSIC IN AMERICA
USIC IN AMERICA M

MUSIC
IN
AMERICA
John Rublowsky

CROWELL-COLLIER PRESS · NEW YORK
COLLIER-MACMILLAN LIMITED · LONDON

Library of Congress Catalog Card Number: 67–25225

The Macmillan Company, New York
Collier-Macmillan Canada Ltd., Toronto, Ontario

Printed in the United States of America

First Printing

PICTURE CREDITS

Columbia Records, 140, 141; Consulate General, Republic of Nigeria, 64–65; Culver Pictures, Inc., 109, 117, 148, 160; Stanley Dance, 136; Historical Pictures Service—Chicago, 15, 24–25, 40, 49, 60, 74, 84, 85, 88, 100, 105, 127; Herman Levin, 171; Museum of Fine Arts, Boston, 18; New York Public Library Picture Collection, 79, 92, 96; Radio Corporation of America, 177; RCA Victor Records, 132, 136, 140, 141; Savoy Record Co. Inc., 140; From the Collection of Dr. Edmond Souchon, 124; The Valentine Museum Collection, Richmond, Va., facing page 1; Yale University Library, 42, 162, 165.

CONTENTS

Sy Gilliat, a Virginia Negro, portrayed in an eighteenth-century painting by an anonymous artist.

1. THE AMERICAN CONTRIBUTION

ARLY in the first decade of the nineteenth century Imperial Russia appointed a certain Count Andreas Rasoumovsky ambassador to the Austrian court in Vienna. By all the standards of his day Count Rasoumovsky was an important personage. Wealthy, influential, he was a man of affairs, a member of that ruling circle whose decisions and actions molded the course of history. In Vienna he established a salon in an elegant palace that became a social and political center.

One of the count's minor interests—no more than a hobby really—was music. He, himself, played the violin enthusiastically, if not very well, and enjoyed performing with groups of similarly minded friends in informal chamber music sessions at his salon. Count Rasoumovsky also considered himself a patron of the arts, as befitted a man of his position and temperament.

With the exercise of a little poetic license we can conjure up a conversation that may have taken place between the count and, let us say, an Austrian baron of his acquaintance who played the cello. The meeting might have taken place in one of Vienna's fashionable coffee houses where the bored and sated aristocracy met to conduct affairs and exchange gossip over coffee and extravagant, whipped-cream-laden pastries. This imaginary conversation might have gone like this:

Count: You must come, my dear baron. Of course, you will bring the cello. I have some new music. One of your local composers wrote it. I commissioned him to put together three quartets with some native Russian themes. He wove them into the music very cleverly. I am sure you will enjoy playing them. Strange fellow, though, this composer. I cannot say that I am completely pleased with the arrangement.

Baron: Why not? Is his music bad?

Count: On the contrary, the fellow is quite talented and very original. His music, though, is devilishly difficult. I asked him to make the parts a bit easier to play, but he refused to change a note. The bounder told me to practice more if I want to play his music.

Baron: He did not! The nerve!

Count: He is arrogant, and surly, and argumentative . . . and his taste in clothing is atrocious. I really cannot say why I put up with the rascal. He is also deaf . . . quite deaf . . . cannot hear a thing.

Baron: A deaf musician? How original of you, Andreas, commissioning a deaf composer! This is amusing. I cannot wait to tell the baroness. What is his name?

Count: He calls himself Ludwig . . . Ludwig Beethoven.

One hundred and fifty years later the count had been forgotten, his name faded by the passage of time. His sole claim to fame remains this commission of three string quartets from a surly, eccentric, deaf composer. Beethoven's Rasoumovsky Quartets, the incomparable Opus 59, brought a measure of immortality to an otherwise undistinguished, obscure Russian count.

We cite this imaginary incident only to show that important accomplishments, those with lasting value, are often overlooked at the time they are made. Count Rasoumovsky would probably have scoffed at the idea that he would be remembered only because of these quartets. Time, however, has an infallible ability to separate the real from the trivial. In this case Beethoven's music proved to be the reality and Count Rasoumovsky, for all his wealth and position, was the triviality.

In this same sense we might speculate on what twentieth-century America will be best remembered for 150 years from now.

There are any number of things that come readily to mind: wealth, perhaps, or the magnificence of our cities; our great industrial capacity or a political ideal. We might be remembered for the concrete ribbons of highway that crisscross and connect all the corners of this nation, or the fleet of great silver jetliners that shrinks our huge expanse of land into hours and minutes. The list is endless. There are so many things to choose from that it becomes almost impossible to make a satisfactory choice.

How many of us would choose music?

At first glance, music would appear to be far down the list of significant American accomplishments; one that would hardly measure up to some of the more spectacular and "important" things. Yet, music may well prove to be one of America's most significant contributions to the twentieth-century world. This may be the accomplishment for which we will best be remembered.

An outlandish idea, perhaps. One that not many people will agree with readily. Still, the accomplishment is there. Since the beginning of the twentieth century American music has exerted a steadily increasing influence on the mainstreams of Western musical expression. We fail to recognize this achievement because it is obscured by a national sense of cultural inferiority.

This sense of inferiority stems, in part, from our history. American music, like all of American culture, is an extension of the European. Our music is based on a historical tradition whose principal lines of development occurred in Old World music centers. As a result Americans have always looked abroad for the finest in music and art. This outlook has become habitual and, like all habits, difficult to overcome. Throughout most of our history native American genius, especially as it manifested itself in music, has either been ignored or looked down on as of little consequence.

Today this attitude is beginning to change. Our national sense of cultural inferiority is fading in the face of accomplishment. American music has played a significant role in twentieth-century development and has been the dominant factor in at least one aspect. For the past fifty years our music has exerted the single most important influence on the popular musical expression of the world. This influence has been so widespread that we can say today that practically the whole world sings an American tune and dances to an American beat.

Actually this influence can be traced back even further in time. America's first musical export was the minstrel show (an indigenous American form the history of which will be traced more fully in a later chapter), which reached a peak in both national and international popularity in the latter half of the nineteenth century. During this period, minstrel shows from America toured the world to delight audiences everywhere with their catchy tunes, sentimentality, and broad humor.

No less a personage than England's Queen Victoria responded to the exuberance and vitality of the minstrel show when she saw a performance in London. William Makepeace Thackeray was another distinguished minstrel fan. The English novelist was so moved by Dan Bryant's impersonation of the hungry old Negro in *Old Time Rocks,* that he described his performance as "one of the finest pieces of tragic acting" he had ever witnessed.

At the turn of the century American ragtime swept over Europe in the wake of the minstrel show. Ragtime had its roots in the minstrel show's flamboyant cakewalk, though it was actually spawned in the honky-tonks and cabarets of St. Louis and Memphis where Negro pianists developed the style with freedom and originality as an indigenous musical expression.

Ragtime rapidly gained immense popularity both in America and abroad. Its syncopated rhythms and sprightly tunes found an enthusiastic audience wherever it was performed, and this enthusiasm quickly assumed the proportions of an international mania. The ragtime craze, which approached the current rock and roll reaction in intensity, saw the dancing habits of the world changed overnight. Within a decade the fox trot replaced the waltz as the favorite ballroom dance and people everywhere were doing the cakewalk.

As a distinctive musical expression, ragtime also captured the interest of European composers who were delighted with the freedom and originality of the form. Claude Debussy, Edward Elgar, Anton Dvořák, and Camille Saint-Saëns were among the eminent composers who utilized ragtime rhythms in their work. This interest came at a time when "serious" musicians in America had nothing but contempt for this "barbaric" outpouring from the dregs of American society. This recognition created one of the first breaches in the wall that separated "popular" and "classical" music in America.

After World War I a second musical invasion occurred. This time it was jazz, a musical style closely related to ragtime. The world began to beat its feet to the syncopated rhythms and improvisational inventions of New Orleans. Here was another native American expression that found a sympathetic audience all over the world. The New World, apparently, had something to say to the Old in a cultural as well as a material sense.

Jazz came into being, essentially, when Negro musicians were able to obtain conventional manufactured instruments. By switching from the banjo and bones—the traditional instruments of the slave warren—to the trumpet, clarinet, and trombone, their range of musical expression was considerably broadened. This new range, in turn, demanded a new idiom.

What began as marching bands soon encompassed ragtime, blues, work songs, and popular dance tunes, and gradually evolved into the expressive, syncopated, improvisational idiom that came to be known as jazz. It developed originally in small New Orleans bands during the 1890's and drew upon the musical originality of such pioneer figures as Charles Bolden, "Bunk" Johnson, Freddie Keppard, Sidney Bechet, and "King" Oliver—to name only a few.

Jazz was quickly recognized throughout the world as a significant musical development. It was looked upon by perceptive musicologists as an expression that was particularly reflective of its moment in time and history. European composers, again, were the earliest champions of the genre, and such outstanding masters as Stravinsky, Milhaud, Ravel, Satie, Prokofiev, and Honegger came under the influence of this vigorous new musical form.

Today American rock and roll has taken possession of stage center as far as popular music is concerned. Like ragtime and jazz before it rock and roll has swept over the world. It is listened and danced to in Japan and Italy, in South Africa and England, in Paris and Copenhagen. Rock and roll provides the dominant theme in today's popular music for America and for the world.

Oddly enough, this all but universal popularity of American music has never been an unmixed source of pride for many Americans. To them it has been and remains a source of embarrassment. This attitude, as we shall see, stems from a schism that has marked the history of American music. This schism has created a gulf between serious and popular music that has plagued American music since the earliest colonial period.

America's musical contribution to the realm of popular expression has been spectacular, and we have not lagged far behind in classical music. Indeed, as we shall see in a later chapter, these two musical strains converged during this century to produce an outpouring of symphonic, operatic, and choral music that rivals the creativity of any other country. In many respects our achievements in art music have paralleled those in popular music.

Today American composers are included in the standard symphonic repertoire, and works by Aaron Copland, Walter Piston, Roy Harris, Charles Ives, George Gershwin, Samuel Barber, Leonard Bernstein, Wallingford Riegger, Alan Hovhannes, Roger Sessions, and others are performed regularly throughout the world. Although their work is steeped in the Western tradition, these composers have evolved a musical language that is reflective of a distinct national expression the roots of which are based in the American experience.

Indeed, it was the recognition of the validity of this experience that stimulated the outpouring of American music in this century. Earlier, serious composers in America looked to the Old World for inspiration. Their work was imitative and eclectic, for the most part, and suffered seriously as a result of these failings.

Another influential aspect of American music lies in the realm of performance. During the past fifty years our symphony orchestras have achieved a level of technical and tonal perfection hitherto considered impossible. Such organizations as the Boston Symphony Orchestra, the Philadelphia Orchestra, the Philharmonic-Symphony Orchestra of New York, the Cleveland Orchestra, and the Chicago Symphony Orchestra have established new standards of performance virtuosity and have played before cheering audiences all over the world.

Part of the credit for this development must go to history. Twentieth-century Europe has been wracked by wars and social unrest. Each crisis has brought an influx of refugees to these shores. Among them were some of Europe's finest musicians, conductors, and composers, who enriched and stimulated American music on all levels.

More important, however, has been the growth of our own schools and conservatories. These have provided a steady supply of musicians whose quality and technical competence have lifted our orchestras to the highest levels. Fifty years ago the serious student of music was compelled to study abroad. Today music students from all over the world flock to American conservatories and schools.

In this second half of the twentieth century American music is flourishing as never before. Hundreds of symphony orchestras play for millions of people all across this land. Our schools and conservatories train and educate the musicians and composers needed to heighten and further this musical activity. In a little more than 350 years America has changed from wilderness to a sophisticated, industrialized nation. Our music has paralleled that development. This book will trace, however briefly, the history of this growth.

2. OF PURITANS AND PSALMS

L ET US go back in time some three hundred years to one of the small villages settled along the coast of Massachusetts Bay by the separatist sect of Puritans called Pilgrims. About 20,000 people lived in the area, in towns with names like Scituate, Duxsbury, Plymouth, Boston, Cambridge, Roxbury, Salem, and Lynn. They built wooden houses with thatched roofs and small windows, and each village was dominated by a church with a steeple that rose higher than any other building. Most of the colonists were farmers but there were also carpenters, blacksmiths, fishermen, and tradesmen among them.

The terrible hardships of the first few years in the wilderness of a New World had been overcome and the Pilgrim communities had begun to acquire a measure of order. New England was beginning to yield its wealth to the disciplined labor of the colonists. Still, the Pilgrims were isolated by vast distances. Behind them stretched a continent and before them was the endless and forbidding North Atlantic. Europe was a grueling three-month journey across the sea.

Their lives were very different from ours today. Travel was limited to the speed of a trotting horse and the enveloping night was relieved only by a sputtering candle. There was no radio, no television, no movies, no theatres, no concerts. There was the church, and people's lives were entwined with the church to an extent that is almost impossible to imagine today. The church was social center, school, government meeting place, and court, as well as the spiritual nucleus of each village.

History has given us a rather unsympathetic portrait of the Pilgrim Fathers. We think of them today as dour, sin-haunted people who looked suspiciously upon all earthly pleasures, whose lives were more involved with the hereafter than the present. This view has been fashioned by generations of writers like Nathaniel Hawthorne who described the Pilgrims in one of his tales as ". . . most dismal wretches, who said their prayers before daylight, and then wrought in the forest or cornfield, till evening made it prayer time again."

This outlook has become part of the mythology of America, leading the American musicologist Frederic L. Ritter to write in his *Music In America*, published in 1883: "The Puritans who landed in 1620 at Plymouth Rock, brought with them their psalm tunes and their hatred of secular music."

Like most stereotypes, this portrait of the dour, ascetic Puritan is somewhat exaggerated. His life may have been church-centered to an extent that is rare today, but the average Puritan was hardly as severe or ascetic as is generally supposed. Contemporary accounts, especially the well-known diary of Judge Samuel Sewall (1652–1730), provide intimate and detailed glimpses into the everyday life of these pioneers. What emerges from these writings is hardly a picture of sin-ridden gloom. Instead we see a people who were very human, who enjoyed good food, good company, and, especially, good music.

Aboard the Mayflower, for example, where space was sorely needed, room was found for the personal library of William Brewster, which included some three hundred volumes of poetry, philosophy, travel, history, and music. And every family aboard that little vessel had its own copy of the Ainsworth Psalter.

The Puritans, it would seem, far from being dour ascetics, were prepared to enjoy some of the "worldly" comforts of life. They brought books of poetry and travel to the New World, along with music books, which many in the congregation were able to read. Edward Winslow, one of the Pilgrim Fathers, in describing the departure of the Pilgrims from Holland, wrote:

> They that stayed at Leyden feasted us that were to go at our pastor's house, being large, where we refreshed ourselves, after tears, with singing of psalms, making joyful melody in our hearts, as well as with the voice, there being many in our

13

congregation very expert in music, and indeed it was the sweetest melody that ever mine ears did hear.

Nor did the Puritans look down on instrumental music, as is commonly believed. Although instrumental music was frowned on in religious worship because it smacked of "popery," it was not forbidden. In the Reverend John Cotton's *Singing of Psalms: A Gospel Ordinance,* written in 1647, it is specifically stated that the "private use of any Instrument of Musick" was not forbidden.

This statement implies the presence of musical instruments in the New England colonies some twenty-seven years after the first landing. How much sooner these instruments came to the New World is a matter of speculation. There is no record of any musical instrument brought aboard the Mayflower although some may have been among the personal effects of the passengers. We do know, however, that instruments were in use from the earliest years of colonization.

Reference to instruments is made in the will of Nathaniel Rogers of Rowley, Massachusetts, dated 1664. It lists a "treble viall" valued at ten shillings. The Rev. Edmund Browne of Sudbury, left a "bass Vyol" and several music books at his death in 1678. The Boston printer and engraver John Foster owned a guitar and a viol, and Judge Sewall writes, in 1690, about his wife's virginal—an early keyboard instrument similar to the harpsichord. Judge Sewall also mentions a Mr. Hiller, a tuner and repairer of musical instruments.

Pages from the Bay Psalm Book, *the first book printed in Massachusetts.*

An advertisement in the *Boston News,* in 1716, announced the arrival of a shipment of instruments from England including "Flageolets, Flutes, Haut-boys, Bass-Viols, Violins, Bows, strings, reeds for Haut-boys, books of instructions for all these instruments, and books of ruled paper. To be sold at the Dancing School of Mr. Enstone in Sudbury Street near the Orange Tree, Boston."

Puritan Boston had a fully equipped music store in a dancing school. From this it would appear that the Puritans were hardly as ascetic as history makes them

15

out to be. The Pilgrim Fathers not only sang psalms in church, but also supported a thriving secular life, entertaining each other with song, instrumental concerts, and even social dancing. Further evidence of this is a dictum handed down by the Reverend John Cotton in 1625, in which he wrote that ". . . Dancing, yea though mixt, I would not simply condemn. . . . Only lascivious dancing to wanton ditties and in amorous gestures and wanton dalliances, especially after great feasts. . . ."

Among the Puritans, however, music—like most other aspects of life—was centered in the church. And central to Puritan church music was the singing of psalms. The New England Pilgrims used a psalm book especially prepared for their congregation, in Holland, by Henry Ainsworth—the famous Ainsworth Psalter, first published in Amsterdam in 1612. This was the music book brought over on the Mayflower. It was the basis for New England church singing throughout the seventeenth century.

The melodies, printed in the customary diamond-shaped notes of the period, and without bar lines, were for one voice only. The complete psalter includes thirty-nine different melodies which Henry Ainsworth attributes to various Old World sources including English, French, and Dutch originals.

Musically the Ainsworth Psalter is of great interest and not only because of historical value. The melodies have considerable metrical variety and rhythmic freedom. Like the music of the New World to which it was brought, the psalter represents a folk tradition that is international in background. The tunes are marked by melodic freedom and rhythmic variety, while retaining a typical folk-music-like freedom of structure.

Neither was the singing of the psalms in the Ainsworth Psalter a solemn affair. Most of the melodies were sprightly and were sung with verve and gusto. So much so, in fact, that Puritan psalm singing gave an impression of liveliness and vigor that led critics of the church to ridicule them as *Genevah Gigs.* Earlier William Shakespeare has one of his characters in *The Winter's Tale* say, "But one Puritan amongst them, and he sings psalms to hornpipes." The hornpipe was a lively sailor's dance.

Music played a far more important role in the lives of the Pilgrim colonists than it does in ours. Music was at once their principal aesthetic experience as well as their chief means of entertainment. Popular entertainment as we know it today was nonexistent. There was only music which provided an accompaniment to practically every activity from church services to barn raisings.

It is not surprising then that the first book printed in the Massachusetts colony was a music book, the famous *Bay Psalm Book.* First printed at Cambridge, Massachusetts, in 1640, it was used by several generations of New Englanders. The last edition was printed in Boston, in 1744, more than one hundred years after the first edition appeared.

In the beginning, Puritan church music was identical with that of its Old World parent body. The original settlers, as we have already seen, were "skilled in musick." Most of them, for example, could read music and follow a score. In church the psalm tunes were sung in a rather lively tempo in unison—so that God would have no difficulty in understanding the words, according to one early commentator. At home, for recreation, the same psalm tunes were often sung in parts with harmonies provided by such seventeenth-century English composers as Ravenscroft and Allison. The principal melody was usually sung by tenors and so-

This virginal, built around 1610, is in the Leslie Lindsey Mason Collection at the Museum of Fine Arts in Boston, by whose courtesy it is reproduced here.

pranos, with the lower voices supplying the harmonies.

In his diary Judge Samuel Sewall describes such a social occasion in an entry dated May 11, 1698: "In the room with the widow Gallis and her daughter Sparhawk; sung the 114th Psalm. Simon catch'd us a base."

Melody, harmony, and singing style, then, were imported from the Old World, along with a certain musical skill which allowed for a fairly polished performance. This comparatively sophisticated style could not, however, survive for long under the harsh conditions of pioneer life. As traditional skills were forgotten or neglected in the face of the urgent needs of merely surviving in this harsh, wilderness environment, music acquired some of the barbarity of the land.

By the middle of the eighteenth century, however, the New England colony had acquired a measure of the order, if not the graces, of civilization together with a distinctly national character. This character revealed itself in music as it did in all aspects of colonial life. During this period New England amateurs produced a thriving musical life. They wrote numerous hymns, metrical psalms, anthems, and "fuguing tunes" (*i.e.,* rounds such as "Row, Row, Row Your Boat") for use both in the church and at home.

This native music, for the most part, was based on recollections of English, German, Dutch, and French reformation originals, but the memory had become somewhat strained and fuddled, so the techniques were clumsy and inexact. These half-intuitive American composers, thinking modally like the folk-singers they were, did not know how to achieve the highly civilized balance between melody, harmony, and counterpoint that characterized European church music at the time.

Yet this rawness, this inexpertness was also their authenticity. A new music was emerging in the New World with a sound unlike anything heard in the Old. The "mistakes" in harmony and counterpoint could, at times, be inspiring. Seen this way, they were not mistakes at all but a creative manifestation of a new identity.

For the first time we thus hear, in the music of the eighteenth century, the rough accents of a New World.

This development led to the first schism in American music. Early in the history of the music of this country we have a manifestation of that polarity which has been such a marked characteristic of subsequent musical developments. On one side were the traditionalists who looked to the Old World and lamented the changes that occurred in the "old sacred melodies." On the other, was the great mass of people who, untutored and unlettered, made music for the sheer joy of the experience. This music reflected and expressed their lives. It developed a distinctive cadence and style that was different from that of the past. The traditionalists sneered at their innovations and dubbed their style with the name "common."

Typical of the traditionalists was the Reverend Thomas Walter (1696–1725) of Roxbury. A graduate of Harvard, with a thorough musical education—by the standards of his time, at least—he wrote an influential text titled *The Grounds and Rules of Musick Explained, or An Introduction to the Art of Synging by Note.* It was printed in Boston, in 1721, by James Franklin (older brother of Benjamin Franklin who was then an apprentice in his brother's shop). Walter's book went through eight editions, the last published in 1764.

"Synging by note" was a term used by the traditionalists to denote the "correct" or "regular" style of singing that they advocated in opposition to "common" singing. In effect it meant singing melodies as they were written, with no variations, additions, or embellishments, and in strict time and pitch.

In his preface to the book, Walter complains of tunes that

> . . . are now miserably tortured, and twisted, and quavered, in some churches, into an horrid Medley of confused and disorderly Noises. . . . Our tunes are, for want of a Standard to appeal to in all our Singing, left to the Mercy of every unskilful Throat to chop and alter, twist and change, according to their infinitely divers and no less odd Humours and Fancies. . . . Our tunes have thus passed through strange Metamorphoses since their first introduction into the New World. . . .

The Reverend Cotton Mather, of Salem Witch Trial fame, also applied himself to the reform of church singing standards. He published a book in 1721, titled the *Accomplished Synger,* intended for:

... the assistance of them that syng psalms with grace in their hearts: but more particularly to accompany the laudable endeavors of those who are learning to syng by Rule, and seeking to preserve a Regular synging in the Assemblies of the Faithful. ...

The winds of change, however, were blowing strongly over the New World. Neither the pietist tradition nor an organized attempt at suppressing musical change succeeded. The Old World "tunes" were destined to pass through strange "metamorphoses" in the New World and there was nothing anyone could do to stop this evolution.

The New England Puritans, then, provided one of the foundations upon which a distinctive American music was to be built. Their music was church-centered and consisted primarily of the singing of psalms, hymns, and anthems that the earliest settlers had brought with them from the Old World. But within a generation these songs began to change under the stresses and influences of a new environment, becoming a distinctly American expression.

Another religious sect which was to have a marked influence upon a developing American music was the *Unitas Fratrum,* or Moravian Brotherhood. This was a Christian communion founded originally in Bohemia, growing out of the reform movement of the martyred John Huss. The sect spread from Bohemia into Saxony in Germany and, early in the eighteenth century, a branch under the leadership of a Count Zinzendorff established colonies in the New World.

Music played a central role in the Moravian communion, which represented a blend of Puritan asceticism with an emotional fervor that was strikingly expressed in their hymns. The Moravians encouraged the study of music, and many of their pastors and lay members were enthusiastic composers. Count Zinzendorff, who led the move to America, was a prolific writer of hymns and is credited with the composition of some 2,000 during his lifetime.

In America the Moravians founded two important settlements, one in Bethlehem, Pennsylvania, and the other in Winston-Salem, North Carolina. At both sites they established a communal society where all worked for the common good and were provided for from a common store. Joined by other Moravians from Europe, the colonies prospered, though they were never very large.

From the point of view of musical activity and influence the Moravians were among the most important of the early religious colonies. The Moravians did not limit their musical activity to the church and encouraged and supported all types of secular music. The Bethlehem colony, for example, could boast of a small orchestra consisting of violins, viola da gamba, viola da braccio, flutes, French horns, haut-boys (oboes), trombones, and a spinet. The orchestra gave regular concerts beginning in 1734, only two years after the Bethlehem colony was first founded.

Then, in December, 1744, the Moravians formed a musical society, the "Collegium Musicum," to encourage the study and performance of chamber music and

The Moravians were an evangelical sect that carried on active missionary work among the Indians. The engraving shows a baptism ceremony.

symphonies. In the performances of the Collegium Musicum, works by such celebrated European composers as Haydn, Mozart, Johann Christian Bach, and Johann Stamitz were first heard in the New World. The Collegium also founded a choir for the performance of oratorios. This group provided the American premières of such choral works as Haydn's *Creation,* Handel's *Messiah,* and *The Israelites In The Desert* by Karl Philipp Emanuel Bach.

The Moravians were primarily an evangelical sect

24

and carried on active missionary work among the Indians and the Negroes who had been brought to the
New World. In 1763 they published a collection of
hymns in the language of the Delaware Indians. They
were also international in outlook and welcomed people from all over the world into their ranks.

On September 4, 1745, a remarkable example of
this aspect of the brotherhood occurred. At a Thanksgiving festival, the hymn, *In Dulce Jubilo,* was sung
in thirteen languages simultaneously: Bohemian,

Dutch, English, French, German, Greek, Irish, Latin, Mohawk, Mohican, Swedish, Welsh, and Wendish. A Dane, a Pole, and a Hungarian were also present at the festivity, but it is not reported whether or not they joined in the singing.

The Moravian colony also developed a notable group of composers during the colonial period. Chief among these was John Frederick Peter (1746–1813) who came to America in 1770 to join the colony in Bethlehem as organist and musical director. Peter was born in Holland of German parents who were members of the brotherhood. He received his early musical training in Holland and Germany.

In 1786 Peter left Bethlehem and was active for several years in Winston-Salem, North Carolina. There he married, and composed the six string quintets upon which his reputation as a composer rests. The quintets were obviously modeled after the classic style of Haydn and Stamitz, though the composer's melodic originality is revealed. When revived for performance today, these works can be listened to with enjoyment of more than their historical significance.

Returning to Bethlehem in 1811, Peter died on July 19, 1813, after a sudden illness. As a teacher and composer he was an important influence in establishing the musical tradition of the Moravian settlements. This tradition has survived to this day. The celebrated Bach Choir of Bethlehem, Pennsylvania—a direct descendant of the original Collegium Musicum of the Moravians—continues to sustain the community's reputation as a music center.

The Moravians, unlike the Puritans, were most influential in the realm of secular music. They brought to the New World a love and respect for the art music that was being created in the Old World during the colonial period. Their orchestras and schools established a tradition of instrumental and performance standards in "serious" music.

Whereas the Puritans and Moravians created a musical expression that was a fundamental influence in the shaping of the music of the New World, the *Ephrata Cloister,* another early American religious community, was something of a musical maverick, interesting today only because of the marked originality of its music.

This colony was established in 1720 along the banks of the Cocalico River in what is now part of Lancaster County, Pennsylvania. Under the leadership of Johann Conrad Beissel and Peter Miller the Ephrata Cloister, or Community of the Solitary as it was also called, established a thriving religious community. They were Seventh-Day Baptists, a pietist Christian sect that believed strongly in music as an aid to worship.

Their music, based upon a system of composition developed by Johann Conrad Beissel, was completely original. A remarkable man in many respects, Beissel was not only founder and leader of the community, but also wrote poetic tracts, sermons, and hymns for their religious services and sang and played several instruments including the violin and harpsichord.

Beissel was born in Eberbach, Germany, of very

7

poor parents. As a youth he learned the baker's trade and was drawn to the Pietists and early Baptists, Christian sects that did not find favor with the German hierarchy of the time. Indeed, his religious views brought him close to an area regarded as heretical in his home country, and Beissel, thirty years old at the time, decided to flee from the intolerance of the Old World and emigrate to America.

Here he worked for a time as a weaver in Germantown and Conestoga, both in Pennsylvania. Then a fresh impulse of religious devotion prompted him to forsake his fellow man and live as a hermit in the wilderness. Soon, however, he found himself the center of a troop of admiring followers and imitators of his way of life.

Unexpectedly, Beissel became the leader of a community, which quickly developed into an independent sect, the Seventh-Day Anabaptists. Beissel ruled the community absolutely, probably because he had never sought leadership, but had had it thrust upon him.

Although Beissel never enjoyed any formal education, he taught himself to read and write and, as leader of the community, developed into a persuasive essayist and pamphleteer. A stream of sermons, didactic prose, and religious songs poured from his pen. His style was florid and cryptic, laden with metaphor and obscure scriptural allusions. A tract on the Sabbath, *Mystyrion Anomalias,* and a collection of ninety-nine *Mystical and Very Secret Sayings,* were among the first writings he prepared for his flock. A series of hymns followed, which were to be sung to well-known

European melodies. They appeared in print under such titles as "Songs For God's Love and Praise," "Zionist Hill of Incense," and "Jacob's Place of Struggle and Elevation."

These collections grew over the years and were finally put together and became the official songbook of the Ephrata Cloister with the flowery title, *Song of the Lonely and Forsaken Turtledove, the Christian Church.*

The songs in this hymnal were meant to be sung, but there was no music. They were merely new texts to old melodies and were so used for many years by the community. But then a new resolve took hold of Beissel. The Ephrata Cloister, he decided, needed a new kind of music which he, as pastor, would provide. No longer young, already far on in the fifties, he applied himself to the problem of working out his own musical system, suited to the special requirements of his people. So successful were this extraordinary man's efforts that before long he had made music the most important element in the religious life of the community.

Most of the church melodies that had come over from Europe seemed to him much too forced, complicated, and artificial to serve his flock. He wanted to do something new, something that would reflect the simplicity of the community and allow these untutored singers to bring it to their own simple perfection.

His solution was bold and ingenious. He decided that every scale should be divided into "master" and "servant" notes. The "masters" would be the notes that make up the common chord of each scale; the rest were "servants." Those syllables of a text upon which the accent fell would be presented by a "master," and the unaccented syllables by the "servants."

Beissel's harmonic process was equally simple and ingenious. He made chord tables for all possible keys. By consulting these tables, any member of the community could write out his tunes comfortably enough in four or even five parts. Rhythmic form, in Beissel's system, simply followed the cadence of the words in the text. Accented syllables were long; unaccented syllables were short. Because he never established a fixed relation between the duration of the long and short notes, this allowed for considerable flexibility in meter which created a free, fluctuating rhythm.

So effective was this system that it generated a rage for composition in the community. Soon there was hardly a single member of the sect, male or female, who had not turned his hand to the composition of hymns and chorals.

Beissel organized the musical life of the community down to the smallest detail. He established choirs, singing and instrumental schools, and even prescribed special diets for different voices—one diet for sopranos, another for altos, and so forth. He also developed a special singing style in which all voices utilized a muted falsetto delivery, with the singers scarcely opening their mouths or moving their lips. The effect was that of a delicate instrumental tone that evoked an impression of heavenly mildness and piety in the listener. This ethereal aspect of the Ephrata choir was com-

mented on by Benjamin Franklin, who printed one
of the editions of the *Turtledove* at his Philadelphia
press.

Beissel's method, though it was original and ingenious, had little effect on subsequent musical development. The community founded by this remarkable
man fell apart after his death. Beissel's music, however, did produce a striking example of "primitive"
art that has won a special niche in the history of American music.

3. MUSIC: SACRED AND SECULAR

A T THE very beginning of colonization the American experience became polarized into two extremes that could never be completely reconciled. On the one hand the New World evoked the highest idealism and the noblest aspirations in the peoples of Europe. On the other, it stimulated naked greed. The opening of the Americas fired the imagination of Europe. There, across the tempestuous sea, was a New World, rich beyond imagining, with land and room for all, and it was waiting for the taking.

In one sense America became Europe's second chance—a divinely provided opportunity to create a new and truly human society, free of the entrenched privilege and moribund conventions of the old. It offered a promise for the fulfillment of that dream of a golden land with justice and freedom for all, which never was and never could be in the Old World. This view is reflected in a poem written in London at the end of the eighteenth century by the English mystic, William Blake:

> Though born on the cheating banks of Thames,
> Though his waters bathed my infant limbs,
> The Ohio shall wash his stains from me:
> I was born a slave, but I go to be free.

But America was an extension of the European consciousness and, along with the idealism, there were projected into the New World all the sins and evils of the Old. We see this side of the coin when we read another remarkable human document, written, at about the same time Blake expressed his vision, by a merchant-financier, not a poet, in another part of London.

This document was addressed to the manager of a Jamaica plantation and dealt with agricultural economy. An objective analysis of the figures compiled in the London countinghouse revealed that an optimum return on their investment could be realized by working a slave to death in seven years. Appropriate suggestions for accomplishing this ideal were forwarded to the manager who, we have no reason to doubt, applied them conscientiously.

So they came to America in an ever-swelling multitude, bands of utopian dreamers alongside hard-headed—and hearted—exploiters. One to create a new Jerusalem in the wilderness, the other to snatch its riches for his own. Often these two extremes were bound up in the same person.

The Puritan who fought bravely for the liberty of his conscience in the Old World found his ideals subtly compromised when he faced the vast emptiness that was America. Here he found opportunity and promise in abundance, guarded only by a backward race of man and his own conscience. The biblical imperative was clear: "Thou Shalt Not Kill."

Faced with this dilemma, Puritan morality shrank in upon itself to allow room for a compromise whose effects were to color the entire subsequent history of the New World. Seizing the land from the "savage" became, in the Puritan mind, an act on behalf of their God. For who but God, they rationalized, placed the Indian—offspring of the devil—in a position so convenient for "divine slaughter at the hands of the English." When Roger Williams, a Puritan of more sturdy conscience than the majority of his fellow Pilgrims, suggested that they buy the land from the Indians, the good Massachusetts settlers reviled and ridiculed him.

Wherever men founded utopian settlements in the New World, and these were numerous in the early days of colonization, the settlers had to face this same dilemma. An element of guilt was injected into the very foundation of their lives. The land upon which they toiled was stolen—a fact that could never be wholly hidden from their consciences even by their most elaborate rationalizations.

This dilemma was expressed in the polarity of the American experience. Because the very foundation of life was erected upon an immorality, the settlers strived mightily to preserve the appearance of morality. Indeed, appearance came to take the place of conviction, making it possible for a freedom-seeking Pilgrim to journey to the New World in a ship the hold of which carried a cargo of black slaves bound, in chains, for those same shores.

This polarization into two extremes became characteristic of the New World and revealed itself throughout the colonial and revolutionary period. The American constitution, for example, represented, at the time it was written, mankind's highest aspiration. Yet it was written and fought for by slave-owners— men who had entered into the most ignoble relationship possible with their fellow men.

America, then, was colonized and settled, in the words of an English fur merchant, "for the greater glory of God—and the advancement of the beaver trade." The two were self-contradictory and this contradiction tore the fabric of colonial life asunder in all of its aspects.

If this polarity tested the consciences of the pioneers, it also affected their music. How could it have been otherwise? In the beginning, music was the sole art available to the settlers. It represented the single human grace that provided solace and release from the considerable care and toil of colonial America. Music was woven into the fabric of life.

The settlers who came over brought with them their folk songs, as well as the religious music which expressed the faith for which they were self-exiled from the comparative safety and comfort of the Old World. But the only music the Puritan settlers could officially tolerate was religious music which they tried vainly, as we have already seen, to preserve from change.

The folk music, however, also survived. Although this kind of musical fare came under the prohibition of the church it never did disappear entirely. We see glimpses of it in records from the earliest periods of colonization. In Salem, Massachusetts, in 1653, Thomas Wheeler was fined for "profane and foolish dancing, singing, and wanton speeches." In July, 1678, Josiah Bridges testified in a court proceeding that "he saw an Indian drunk on brandy and cider" in the home of a Mr. Crod, where he also saw "music and dancing when it was pretty late." In 1679 a Mary Indicott of Salem complained that she saw "fiddling and dancing in John Wilkinson's house."

These court records show that there was fiddling and dancing and profane singing among the people of New England, even though it was officially prohibited. Most of this music came from England, where a music book published in 1651, titled *The English Dancing Master,* can give us some idea of the type of popular song that was then in vogue. Included in the collection were such famous songs as "Green Sleeves," "Selinger's Round," and "Trenchmore," which had circulated in an oral tradition long before they were set down in print. We can be certain that the people of the American colonies knew them well.

Despite all official prohibitions this folk music survived. It was handed down orally from generation to generation, changed, and became one of the sources from which an indigenous American music was to grow.

Thus we see this polarity revealed from the very beginning of colonization. Its first expression created a gulf between sacred and secular music. One was encouraged and preserved while the other was looked down on and prohibited. Nor was this polarity limited to the Puritan settlements of New England. It was also revealed in the music of the Moravian Brotherhood which attempted to preserve musically, as well as in every other way, a home away from home. The Moravians showed no desire to create a new musical world and remained content to cultivate the old. They had transported their European culture, along with their way of life, to the New World and resisted all change and originality.

Only the music of the Ephrata Cloister rejected the old musical forms in an attempt to create a new expression for a New World. But this attempt was stillborn. The music of the Cloister, as well as the community, depended too strongly upon the charisma of one man, Johann Conrad Beissel. Neither community nor music survived for long after his death.

We see an attitude taking shape from the earliest period of American history that separated music into two conflicting spheres. At first this division was made between sacred and secular music. Then, as the hardships and tribulations of the first period of settlement gave way to a more ordered life, this attitude changed subtly, but remained split into two poles.

By the mid-eighteenth century a new society had

evolved in America. In the North it was made up of
yeoman farmers, tradesmen, and a rapidly growing
merchant class. In the South it developed around a
tradition that arose from different conditions. Here
huge plantations came into being, worked, for the
most part, by imported Negro slaves. These plantations supported a New World elite whose wealth and
position enabled it to emulate a European aristocratic
tradition.

During this phase of the colonial period southern
wealth and leisure turned to the cultivation of the
arts. Music and musicians were imported from the
Old World to grace the social life of this new elite.
The South, then, became the center of musical life in
the New World, and Charleston, South Carolina, was
one of the principal centers of the South.

Here the city fathers established the St. Cecilia Society in 1762 for the "encouragement of the arts of
music and for the sponsorship of musical concerts."
The society combined private subscription concerts
with the most elegant and exclusive social amenities.
One such concert, sponsored by the society, was described by Josiah Quincy of Boston, who visited
Charleston in 1772. His account of the affair offers a
glimpse into the music and manners of the eighteenth-
century South:

> The music was good . . . the two bass viols and
> French horns were grand. One Abercrombie, a
> Frenchman just arrived, played the first violin, and
> a solo incomparably better than any one I ever
> heard. . . . There were upwards of 250 ladies pres-

ent and it was called no great number. . . . The gentlemen, many of them dressed with richness and elegance, uncommon with us: many with swords on. We had two macaronis present, just arrived from London.

This reference to "macaronis" throws an interesting light on the proceedings. Macaroni was the Yankee word for the dandified English fops of the time who evoked an ambivalent response from the colonists. They were looked up to as the ultimate arbiters of taste and fashion, on the one hand, and looked down on as frivolous and extravagant, on the other. This attitude was reflected in the famous revolutionary war song, "Yankee Doodle Dandy":

He stuck a feather in his cap and called it macaroni.

This was all part of the general pattern of eighteenth-century American culture. Among those who could afford it there was a deep-felt desire to imitate European taste and manners. This tendency was, basically, an expression of the newly generated wealth of the New World. A wealthy class had emerged in America and, like the *nouveau riche* everywhere, they wanted the "best" of everything—from fiddlers to English fops.

Among this new class was an enthusiastic group of fine amateur musicians. Emulating European standards of the time, social usage made it imperative for a "gentleman" or "lady" to be able to play a musical instrument. Consequently, a steady stream of good European instruments found their way into the manor

Ladies and gentlemen strived to master European musical techniques in the eighteenth century.

houses of the New World, where ladies and gentlemen spent a considerable amount of time mastering their techniques.

Typical of this kind of gentleman amateur was Robert Carter of Nomini Hall in Virginia. An account of the musical life of this distinguished Virginia house was written by Vickers Fithian, a tutor who worked for the household before the Revolutionary War. Mr. Carter, Fithian wrote, "has a good ear for music, a vastly delicate taste and keeps good instruments; he has here at home a Harpsichord, Forte Piano, Harmonica, Guitar & German Flute. . . . he himself also is indefatigable in the practice. . . ."

A more distinguished "gentleman amateur" was

Thomas Jefferson of Monticello, Virginia. As a student at the College of William and Mary in Williamsburg, Virginia, he became an intimate friend of Francis Fauquier, Lieutenant Governor of the Virginia colony, through his musical abilities. Jefferson played the violin and was thus welcomed into that music-loving circle that had developed around the lieutenant governor.

Nor was this taste for music limited to the comparatively wealthy South. Throughout the colonies those who could afford the practice diligently studied music. John Penn, Lieutenant Governor of Pennsylvania from 1763 to 1771, was an enthusiastic music lover and a fine violinist who arranged chamber-music concerts at his home in Philadelphia. These concerts were a regular Sunday night feature attended by most of the leading families of Philadelphia.

Another Philadelphian of note who showed marked interest in music was Benjamin Franklin. Franklin played the guitar and harp and revealed a thorough musical knowledge and exceptional taste in his many letters that deal with music. The Philadelphia printer also invented an instrument that enjoyed considerable vogue for a time throughout the world. This was the *Harmonica,* an arrangement of tuned glasses of different size without stems. These glasses were placed on a horizontal spindle which was rotated by foot action. The instrument was played by sitting in the middle of the set of glasses, as before a keyboard, turning them with the foot while keeping the rims wet with a sponge.

41

So successful was Franklin's musical invention that it attracted the attention of the leading composers of the time. Wolfgang A. Mozart, for example, wrote two compositions for the harmonica: a Quintet (Adagio and Rondo) for harmonica, flute, oboe, viola and cello (Köchel 617), and an Adagio for harmonica solo (Köchel 356). Ludwig van Beethoven and Robert Schumann also wrote music for the instrument.

Although music was held in high esteem by the colonists, professional musicians were not considered gentlemen. This distinction was made clear in advertisements for concerts and performances of the time. Since there were few communities in America that could support enough professionals to make up a full orchestra, "gentlemen" amateurs were often called

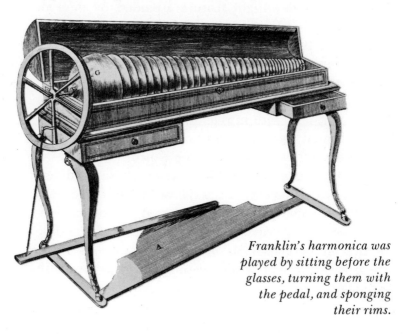

Franklin's harmonica was played by sitting before the glasses, turning them with the pedal, and sponging their rims.

upon to lend their talents and abilities to public concerts. A typical announcement from the Pennsylvania Gazette of Philadelphia, November 30, 1769, described such a concert: "The orchestra . . . will be assisted by some musical Persons, who as they have no View but to contribute to the Entertainment of the Public, certainly claim a Protection from any Manner of Insult." Insult, in this case, refers to the time-honored custom of pelting those who fail to please with decayed fruit and vegetables.

We can see, then, from contemporary accounts that have come down to us from the colonial and revolutionary period that America supported a surprisingly sophisticated musical life. In the stately homes of the newly-emerged wealthy classes, musical skill came to be a mark of both acceptance and status. These private salons and concert halls were well acquainted with all the important European composers of the time. Here the works of Handel, Haydn, Vivaldi, Corelli, Boccherini, Rameau, Mozart, Stamitz, K. P. E. Bach, and later, Beethoven, were played and listened to not very long after they were first performed in Europe.

During this period, also, a steady stream of accomplished musicians made their way to the New World. Here they performed and taught and composed music in the style and forms of their European contemporaries. The result, at least along the Eastern Seaboard, was a musical life that compared favorably, in terms of the variety of music heard if not in the quality of performance, with that of the European musical centers of the time.

We can also see from these accounts a stiffening of the attitude that separated music into two mutually exclusive camps in the earliest colonial period. A genteel tradition was established during this period that was to color all of American music throughout the nineteenth century. What had been polarized in terms of sacred and secular now became even more pronounced in terms of genteel and common.

Genteel music was that which came from Europe, whether the "art" music of the important Old World composers or the songs from the music halls of England and France. Common music was that which the ordinary people practiced: the rough, vigorous songs of the frontiersmen; the sea chanteys of the growing American naval forces both civilian and military; the work shouts, field hollers, and religious songs of the slave warren; the folk music of the Swedish, Danish, German, Scotch, and Irish settlers who came in ever-increasing numbers to the Americas.

Most of what we know from this period comes down to us from newspapers and private journals which dealt, for the most part, with only one stratum of society. There is a great deal written about the elegant concerts given in colonial Williamsburg, Virginia, but very little about the music that was practiced along the frontier or in the poor taverns and music halls of the established eastern cities.

The principal reason for this neglect was the fact that this music was looked down on as low and vulgar by the upper classes of society. This kind of break between "art" and "common" music was a peculiarly

American phenomenon. In Europe, art music evolved naturally from the great body of folk music of the different national regions. European composers borrowed freely from the music of the people, incorporating popular songs and dances into their works. Haydn, Handel, Mozart, Beethoven, all the composers of the classic period had their musical roots firmly planted in the broad body of their respective national backgrounds. The later romantic composers deliberately sought out a folk tradition for their musical expression.

In America, however, music was a house divided. The arbiters of taste had decreed an arbitrary boundary separating music into conflicting camps—"art" on one hand, and "vulgarity" on the other. A tradition of musical appreciation and sophistication was established in the New World, but at the expense of anything new and original that this world might·produce.

The music of the people was ignored or ridiculed as crude and common. Yet it was the rough song of the backwoodsman and the plaintive chant of the lowly Negro slave that was to become, in time, the indigenous voice of America. A true musical creativity was beginning to reveal itself during this period. An American voice was being born—but not in the elegant manor houses of Virginia.

4. SONG OF THE GREAT FOREST

WHEN SETTLERS from England first arrived in the New World in the early seventeenth century, that part of North America which was destined to become the United States was sparsely populated by an estimated 1,500,000 Indians. This population was broken up into a bewildering number of different tribes, each with its own language, customs, and traditions.

Most of the North American tribes were small. The Mohawks, for example, who played such an important role in the colonial period, numbered no more than 12,000 individuals at the height of the tribe's population. This was considered a large tribe. In fact, the Mohawks were the largest tribe in the Northeast. Most of the tribes were much smaller. More typical were the Mohicans who lived in parts of what is now Westchester County and nearby Connecticut, and never numbered more than 2,000 individuals.

The eastern Indians encountered by the early English settlers were of mixed Algonquian and Iroquoian stock (these refer to linguistic groups rather than confederations). Within each group there were numerous independent tribes. Only the five Iroquois nations—the Cayuga, Mohawk, Oneida, Onondaga, and Seneca tribes—had joined together into anything resembling a federation.

These tribes lived, for the most part, by hunting; cultivation of corn, squash, and beans; fishing; and the gathering of wild nuts, fruits, and berries. Their stage of economic and cultural development was roughly equivalent to that of the earliest Neolithic period—a stage the ancestors of the European settlers had gone through some four or five thousand years earlier.

This contact between a backward and comparatively advanced people was a tragic encounter for the Indians. Diseases introduced by the Europeans against which the Indians had no natural resistance, such as smallpox and tuberculosis, took a frightful toll of their numbers. In early accounts by the Puritans, there are descriptions of Indian villages where the entire population was killed off by these diseases.

The superior weapons of the settlers took a further toll of Indian life. So severe was this attrition that within two hundred years after the arrival of the English, Indian culture and society in the Northeast was all but obliterated.

Most of the Indian tribes were semisedentary. That is, they erected villages and cultivated farms, but these

47

were, at best, semipermanent arrangements. As game grew scarce or the land became unproductive, the Indians merely packed their few possessions and moved to a more promising site.

Their temporary settlements were often palisaded as a protection against raids by neighboring tribes. Intertribal warfare was a characteristic feature of their life. Within the palisade the Indians lived in long houses, each of which sheltered a maternally lineated clan that often included as many as twenty-five individual families, with painted crests depicting the clan on the gabled ends.

A village band of several hundred persons was the economic and social unit in this forest culture. Occupations were sharply divided between the sexes. Gangs of men built houses, erected palisades, fished, hunted, traveled, traded, participated in elaborate intertribal games, defended the village, and made war on neighboring tribes. Women did all of the farming, made clothing, wove baskets and containers, and looked after the children.

The long house was the basic unit of Indian society. These households of blood lineage were projected into clans, clans into moities, moities into tribes or nations. Kinship and loyalty were the basis for political life. Each community had its council of adult males, chosen by the people of the village, who guided the village chiefs. There were chiefs for various aspects of tribal life. The Peace Chief, for example, was concerned with civil affairs of the village and was chosen by the women.

Music was an indispensable part of Indian ceremonies such as this prayer session.

Speakers of the council were called Pine Tree Chiefs and had earned the right to voice their opinions at council meetings through merit exhibited in hunting or warfare. In forest protocol, the speakers elected the hierarchy of Hunting and War Chiefs.

The Indians appear to have been partial to councils and spent an inordinate amount of time at these meetings. One of these tribal meetings was described by J. F. Lafitau, a French Jesuit, who lived among the Mohawks during the latter part of the seventeenth century:

> ... a greasy assemblage, the braves sitting on their haunches, crouched like apes, their knees as high as their ears, or lying, some on their backs, some on their stomachs, each with a pipe in his mouth, discussing affairs of state with as much coolness and gravity as the Spanish Junta or the Grand Council of Venice. ...

Like all primitive people their lives were circumscribed by ceremony. There was a ceremony for every occasion from the beginning of a hunting expedition to the election of chiefs, from the planting of maize to the birth of a child, from the preparations for war to the council of peace. Music was an indispensable part of each ceremony.

So pervasive was music in the lives of the Indians that this characteristic has been noticed by all who came into contact with them. Natalie Curtis, who studied Indian life and wrote an influential book on their culture, published in 1907, described the role of music in Indian life like this:

Wellnigh impossible it is for civilized man to conceive of the importance of song in the life of the Indian. To the Indian, song is the breath of the spirit that consecrates the acts of life. Not all songs are religious, but there is scarcely a task, light or grave, scarcely an event, great or small, but has its fitting song. . . .

Alice C. Fletcher, another student of Indian life, wrote in 1893:

Music enveloped the Indian's individual and social life like an atmosphere. There was no important personal experience where it did not bear a part, nor any ceremonial where it was not essential to the expression of religious feeling. The songs of a tribe were coextensive with the life of the people.

It is not surprising that so musical a people responded to the music brought over by Europeans. An account of this response comes to us in the journal of Francis Fletcher, chaplain aboard the ship in which Sir Francis Drake circumnavigated the globe in 1577. In June, 1579, the ship anchored off the coast of what is now northern California, where it stopped for some five weeks while the crew made repairs and took on provisions. The Indians of the area proved friendly and frequently visited the English camp. Fletcher described these visits:

In the time in which prayers, singing of Psalmes, and reading of certaine Chapters in the Bible, they sate very attentively: and observing the end of every

pause, with one voice still cried, Oh, as greatly re-
joycing in our exercises. Yea, they took such pleasure in our singing of Psalmes, that whensoever they
resorted to us, their first request was commonly this,
Gnaah, by which they intreated that we would sing.

This Indian responsiveness to western music is
credited with saving the Moravian settlement in Bethlehem, Pennsylvania, soon after the colony was established in the eighteenth century. The story goes that
during the French and Indian War a war party of
Mohawks was planning to attack the settlement and
lay in wait until the coming of darkness. But before
they could attack, a chorus of trombones began to
play a dirge for the death of one of the brethren. The
Indians, according to the tradition, were so moved by
the sounds of the music that they gave up the attack.

More surprising than Indian responsiveness to European music is the fact that Indian music has left so
little imprint upon subsequent developments. Settlers
lived in intimate contact with Indians throughout the
history of the New World. Indian words, customs, and
techniques were borrowed by the settlers freely. Yet
Indian music has had practically no influence on American music.

Only in Mexico, Peru, Chile, and Ecuador did the
native Indian music leave a recognizable influence in
the musical developments of those countries, an influence which is conspicuously absent in the rest of the
New World. In these areas, the Indians had evolved a
much higher level of culture than had been achieved
in the rest of the hemisphere. This level was ex-

Mexican Indian music was highly developed before the arrival of the Spaniards.

pressed, of course, in musical terms as well as in all other aspects of their civilizations.

Music was highly developed in the great Incan, Aztec, and Mayan civilizations, all of which supported schools and a population of professional musicians. In these schools instruments were studied and perfected along with the techniques and forms of musical composition. This music became incorporated into the national music of the new countries that came into being in those areas. North American Indian music, on the other hand, has left little imprint on subsequent musical life.

To understand the reasons for this restricted influence, we must examine the structure and forms of North American Indian music. Unfortunately, the first serious studies of Indian music were not undertaken until the latter half of the nineteenth century. Thus, we have no reliable descriptions of earlier musical expression. What accounts we do have, describe a music that is totally different from that of the European tradition.

Modern musicologists confirm this view. Their studies show that there was no conception of scales, modes, or tonality in Indian music. Indeed, their songs were really no more than chants the effect of which is achieved through a droning repetition of tonal patterns sung against a rhythmic background provided by gourds and drums. The rhythmic concept also falls into a repetitive pattern with a single pulse or rhythmic figure simply repeated throughout the performance of the song. There is no recurring metronomic accent as in the European and African tradition. In many respects this expression is similar to the Hindu and Bhuddist chants, or *Mantras,* which consist of limited musical phrases repeated against a steady rhythmic pulse. The hypnotic effect of this kind of musical expression can be testified to by anyone who has ever listened to these chants.

Most Indian melodies fall into a pentatonic, or five-tone, scale. They were sung as solos or in unison by groups of singers. There was, consequently, no concept of harmony or counterpoint. A Seneca harvest song—the Senecas were one of the five nations in the Iroquois federation—which was transcribed by Theodore Baker who studied this music in the 1870's, is typical of the type of song that the early English settlers heard in the New World.

The melody contains only four notes, G, B, D, and E, which were sung by men to the accompaniment of rattles and drums. The melody contains many repeated tones and the melodic line often drops a fifth—apparently a favored interval in Indian music. The metrical pattern is irregular with only one figure repeated with any regularity throughout the performance. This song was often sung for an hour or more at a stretch.

Singing style was also very different from that of the European tradition. There was, for example, a continuous slurring of one note into another. A practice which, when combined with the marked vibrato of Indian singing, sounded discordant and chaotic to the western ear. This effect became even more pronounced as the result of the Indian practice of pulsating the voice, creating a rhythm within the rhythm of the song.

Important as this music was to the life of the Indian, it was too different in both concept and performance to be absorbed into the European tradition. It stemmed from a primitive culture that had nothing in common with the norms and trends of a developing American civilization.

There was, however, a romantic revival that spurred an interest in Indian tribal music during the first decades of the twentieth century. At this time a number of American "art" composers, searching for a distinctive American theme for their compositions, delved into the all-but-forgotten Indian tradition. The result was not particularly gratifying, either as pure music or as a revival of Indian music.

Included in this group of "Indianists" was Henry Gilbert (1868–1928) who summed up his musical credo in a foreword printed with the score of his symphonic poem "The Dance in Place Congo":

> It has been . . . an ideal of mine to write music which should be in its inspiration native to America. The efforts of my compatriots, though frequently very fine technically, failed to satisfy me. To my mind they leaned far too heavily upon the tradition of Europe, and seemed to me to ignore too completely the very genuine touches of inspiration which exist in our history, our temperament, our national life. . . .

Gilbert's five "Indian Scenes" for piano stem from this concern. Charles Wakefield Cadman (1881–1946) was another composer who delved into Indian music. One of his songs "The Land of the Sky Blue Water," supposedly based upon an Indian song, achieved wide popularity, though its saccharine melodic and harmonic treatment had very little in common with anything Indian. Cadman also composed two operas on Indian themes, one of which, *Shanewis,* was produced at the Metropolitan Opera House in New York in 1918.

Charles Sanford Skilton (1868–1941) is another composer in this group. Skilton became strongly attracted to Indian music while teaching at the University of Kansas in 1915. This interest was expressed in several operas and orchestral suites on Indian themes, which enjoyed a considerable vogue and were widely performed for a time.

This romantic movement represents a transitory phase in the development of American music. Indian music attracted the attention of a number of American composers who were searching for something indigenous and native. Indian music, however, proved to be a blind alley. Tribal music had never been a part of the mainstream of American culture and it was impossible to force it into this role at so late a date.

Today we study Indian music as an example of a primitive musical expression superbly adapted to the needs and aspirations of the people who developed this mode. The conditions that led to this particular development have disappeared and it is unlikely that they will ever return.

5. A PEOPLE IN BONDAGE

IN THE YEAR 1619, one year before the Pilgrims landed at Plymouth Rock, a Dutch ship dropped anchor off the English colony of Jamestown, Virginia. It was a merchant vessel that carried a cargo of goods and materials for trade with the New World. Included in the manifest were a number of Negro slaves who were purchased by the colonists to labor in perpetual servitude.

Thus began one of the most extraordinary migrations in world history. This first trickle of human cargo swelled into a wave. By the Revolutionary period there were some 750,000 Negroes in America out of a total population of 4,000,000. When the American Civil War began this number had grown to well over 4,500,000. It is estimated that between 1620 and 1850 some 15,000,000 Negro slaves were imported into the New World, the largest number being taken to South America and the Caribbean Islands.

Unlike the great bulk of the white population of the New World the Negro did not come to America in search of either freedom or opportunity. He came as a slave. He came as another man's "property." He came in chains, forcibly uprooted from his traditions and culture.

In fact his culture was deliberately obliterated. The slavemaster was, of necessity, a shrewd practical psychologist. Pragmatic experience taught him the value of this cultural destruction. Culture makes a man bigger than his individual self. Take away that culture and you take away a large part of the man. What is left is a raw individual upon whom all the formative powers of the whip and chain can be exercised.

Families were separated; friends were taken from each other; fellow tribesmen were carefully and systematically segregated. In this way, the Negro came to these shores stripped of his past. The past is more than memory. It is shared experience and mutual tradition and history. These were forcibly taken away and the Negro was compelled to create a new tradition, a new myth in place of his obliterated past.

In building this new tradition the creativity of the Negro centered primarily upon music. The Negro became a kind of New World catalyst, combining the various strains that came to the Americas into an indigenous musical expression. So influential has this creativity been that today it pervades all American music. Dig deep enough into practically any aspect of American music and you will find that the music of the American Negro is at its source.

The Negro, stripped of his culture, turned to music for solace in the slave quarters.

The Negro was transported to America under the worst possible circumstances. He faced the New World stripped of his freedom and his past. He turned to music for solace and release from an intolerable situation. It was a choice based on necessity, since other forms of creative activity, which soften the trials of existence, were denied him.

The visual arts were out of reach despite an African tradition of sculpture, painting, and design that rivaled that of any other culture. This art exerted a profound influence on western expression when it became available to European artists in the nineteenth century. But for the slave the visual arts were beyond aspiration. It takes a certain amount of leisure to develop the necessary skills, and funds to procure tools and materials. Neither of these was available to the Negro slave.

Similar limitations prevented any development in literature. It was against the law to permit a slave to learn how to read and write, and without these basic skills it becomes almost impossible to create a literature. The Negro did, however, develop a rich oral poetry which we are only now beginning to appreciate. This poetry has worked its way into the language as a pithy "slang" idiom which has become part of American oral expression.

This "plagiarism" was commented upon recently by Del Shields, a Negro disc jockey from Philadelphia, who complained that:

> . . . radio has adopted most of the slang, the "hip" phrases, programming policies of the Negro stations. In fact, the general stations owe their slam-bang approach success to Negro radio. . . .

The art inherent in the history and mythology of America was also denied the Negro, though for a different reason. History is art to the extent that it is colored and modified by the wish-factor in the population of a specific country. The history of America is very different as taught in England or the Soviet Union from what it is when taught in America.

The patriotic slogans, the heroes that Americans revered, had a hollow ring in the ear of the slave. He could not venerate the memory of a George Washington or a Thomas Jefferson. He knew that they owned slaves. They bought and sold human beings. The attitude of the Negro slave toward the traditions and myths of American history was necessarily different from that of the slave master.

This attitude was expressed in a poem by the Negro poet Langston Hughes:

> Let's make America America again
> Not that it ever was.

The American Negro was left with only one artistic channel into which to funnel his creative energies— music.

Basically, music needs no more than the human body for expression. Everyone has a voice and can sing, and everyone can clap his hands or beat his feet. These activities provide the two fundamentals of music— rhythm and melody. Leisure time is not necessary. One can sing while working. Hard physical labor is even made easier by singing.

Although his cultural heritage and traditions were systematically destroyed by the slave master, the Negro retained the memory of a rich musical tradition. This retention revealed itself in the modifications that the Negro in America made on the secular and religious music practiced by the white population of the New World. It was demonstrated in a special type of singing, in the call and response pattern of the work song and field holler, in the supple harmonies of the religious songs the Negro sang.

Musicologists have traced this tradition to the musical forms and styles of West Africa, the region from which most American Negroes derive. Rhythmic and harmonic patterns of African music bear a direct relationship to the music of the American Negro to this day.

Severely restricted in his aspirations by a cruel and immoral condition, the despised and exploited black man turned to music. Since his creative energies were channeled into a single area, it is not surprising that the Negro in America demonstrated a marked musicality.

Not only were his inherent musical abilities highlighted, but his selective sense was also sharpened and enhanced. The slave came to music in an innocent state—innocent in the sense that music served a purely creative function in his life. He was not concerned with any snobbish or national appeal, nor did he consider music an individual adornment—a cultural attainment with which to impress his neighbors. For him, music was a means of survival, nothing less. Music was a collective expression in which the entire community participated. It was solace and inspiration —that art which, above all others, made the unbearable life of the slave bearable.

This marked feeling for musical expression was recognized from the first introduction of slaves into the New World. It was remarked on by Thomas Jefferson, who wrote in his *Notes on Virginia:*

> In music they [Negroes] are generally more gifted than whites, with accurate ears for tune and time and they have been found capable of imagining a small catch. . . .

Nigerian musicians: rhythmic and harmonic patterns of African music bear a direct relationship to the music of the American Negro.

This "small catch" was destined to have a deeper influence upon American music than Jefferson, reflecting the pervasive racism of his day, ever dreamed possible.

One of the factors that led to this influence was the fact that African music is closely related to European. The diatonic scale, for instance, is common to both. It is the strongest link between the two musics and is the characteristic that distinguishes them from all other musical systems. Then there is a basic concept

of harmony shared by African and European music,
though this factor was more highly developed in the
European tradition.

The African concept of rhythm, however, was more
complex and sophisticated than the European. In
European music different rhythms may have been
used successively, but rarely at the same iime. A characteristic of African music was a simultaneous use of
many different rhythmic patterns.

A typical example from Dahomey, on the coast of

West Africa, may have incorporated three, sometimes four or five, different rhythmic patterns expressed in one musical statement. A common combination, still in use all over West Africa, has two percussion parts, one of which may be the clapping of hands in addition to a drum, played against a vocal section with its own rhythmic pattern. Often, in more formal performance, there are a number of metrical patterns in percussion, each played on a drum of different size and timbre. Chaos is avoided by the presence of an underlying beat that remains constant. Rhythm in African music is conceived of as a combination of different time patterns that all coincide at regular intervals. This metronomic beat is also characteristic of European music.

These factors, which were exhaustively studied and described by the musicologists Kolinski and Watermann, reveal the relationship between European and African music. These common factors, in turn, facilitate the process of musical synthesis or blending when the two musical systems are brought into contact with each other over a long period of time. This is what happened in America, and it explains the homogeneous character of American Negro music.

The Negro, then, acted as a musical catalyst in America. He borrowed freely from the music he heard in the New World, from hymns and psalms as well as secular songs and dances. Because of his innocence he was able to select those aspects that had true musical value. This music, in turn, was enriched by his own African heritage and the whole thing was perfected and enhanced by a severely restricted creative energy.

Musical gold was being refined in the crucible of the slave warren. It was not long before others recognized its value.

The influence of African music was noted as early as 1753. A description of a Richmond ball that was printed in the *Virginia Gazette* describes the music of Sy Gilliat and London Briggs, two Negro musicians who "belonged" to the household of Baron Botetourt, later Governor General of the colony:

> . . . to the music of Gilliat's fiddle and Brig's flute, all sorts of capers were cut . . . sometimes a *Congo* was danced and then the music grew fast and furious when a jig climaxed the evening. . . .

The congo, which was described by Lafcadio Hearn more than a hundred years later, after seeing it danced by Negroes in New Orleans in 1858, was nothing more than a modified version of an African tribal dance that was performed by Negroes throughout the eighteenth and nineteenth centuries all over the New World. It is interesting to note that a version was also performed by the dandies of colonial Virginia society.

At the beginning of the nineteenth century this influence, which was only hinted at in this eighteenth-century account, became obvious. Its first really national expression came with the immensely popular minstrel show, which dominated American popular music throughout the nineteenth century.

Negro music in America evolved in two distinct phases, the roots of which can be traced to the colonial period. One phase developed out of secular music—a

67

coming-together of English, Scotch-Irish, German, and French songs and dances that were transformed and enriched by African influences.

This can be traced from a West African harmonic and rhythmic tradition to plantation songs and field hollers, to the minstrel show, then through ragtime and on into jazz. All along this line of development additions and modifications were constantly being made. These came about through the influence of the popular stage and commercial considerations, as well as through technical considerations that involved instruments and performance techniques.

Many of these developments and modifications were the result of activities by white musicians and performers. But the source is unmistakably Negro and this influence is plainly recognized in the works of such white composers as Stephen Foster, George Gershwin, Irving Berlin, and even Richard Rodgers.

The second phase of this musical development evolved through the activities of the church. The synthesis of African traditions with primarily Anglo-Saxon church music gave birth to the spiritual with all its ramifications in the blues and Negro gospel singing.

Again we can trace a direct line of development that runs from the West African call-and-response chant to American Negro work songs and field hollers, to the spiritual, to gospel singing, and finally, to today's rock and roll. If jazz can be considered the secular expression of the American Negro, then rock and roll must be considered an expression of his religious life—an echo of that "joyous shout unto the Lord" voiced by the indomitable spirit of a sorely oppressed and abused people.

Another pattern of influence on American music also derives from the experience of the Negro in the New World. This genesis took place in South America and the Caribbean Islands, notably Jamaica and Cuba, and is known today as Latin American music.

Developing under similar conditions, this music is the result of a synthesis of African with Spanish and Portuguese traditions. American Negro music represents a blend of African with primarily Anglo-Saxon traditions. The fact that both Afro-Cuban and Latin American music found such a responsive audience in North America can be attributed to this common source.

It is interesting to note that Mexican music has had very little influence on American expression despite the proximity of the two countries. Mexico never had a sizable Negro population and Mexican music, consequently, remained primarily Spanish with an element of Indian music. As a result this music lacked a common base to facilitate a response in the American audience.

The American Negro, then, has made a primary contribution to the creation of an indigenous American musical expression. It is his song we sing today, and his rhythms to which we dance.

This is a music that has been some 300 years in the making. It is a music that was once a question of life and death—nothing less. To understand this fact we must go back to the Negro slaves who brought this music to the Americas. An estimated twenty million died in the passage from Africa, and the survivors who reached these shores were as close to being dead as any forcibly transported people in history.

All this dying was bad for business. A live slave was a negotiable asset, a dead one was worthless. The slave traders, being practical men, tried everything to stem this disastrous mortality rate. They gave the slaves good red beans to eat and clean water to drink. They gave them, at times, better living quarters than those of the crew, but still their cargo insisted on dying.

Then someone discovered that if you made slaves sing and dance they stayed alive. Just plain exercise was no good. It had to be the lindy, the rhumba, and the twist—only the real originals. It was this that led Thomas Starks, a London merchant in the slave trade, to write the captain of the bark *Africa,* in 1700, which had taken on a cargo of 450 slaves from the Gold Coast: "Make your Negroes cheerful and pleasant, making them dance at the beating of the drum. . . ."

It is this music, modified and altered through countless evolutionary changes, that has given the distinctive character to American music. It gave birth to ragtime and jazz, to the rhumba and the samba, to gospel song and rock and roll. It represents the single most significant cultural contribution made to this country by any minority group. The Negro taught America how to sing and dance and today the whole world has taken up this beat.

6. *MADRIGALS IN APPALACHIA*

BY THE MIDDLE of the eighteenth century the Eastern Seaboard had been fairly well settled. While life was still rough and crude, especially on the frontier, those who lived in the established coastal cities and towns were beginning to enjoy some of the order and comforts of settled life. The rude huts and log cabins of the early settlers were being replaced by handsome, sturdy wood and stone homes and many mansions had been erected before 1776. Food was abundant and varied, with the produce of farms generously supplemented by rich fisheries and abundant game.

By this time, also, a native aristocracy had emerged in the new land. In the New England colonies, where geographic conditions did not allow for extensive landholding, this aristocracy was determined, for the most part, by commercial success. In the South, however, ownership of land and slaves determined social position.

In the decade preceding the Revolutionary War, the principal element in the population of the colonies was English, although the mixing of various national strains that was to become such a characteristic feature of America had already begun. The New England colonies were almost exclusively English, as were the southern colonies. The Middle Atlantic States had already attracted sizable colonies of Dutch, Swedish, German, and Bohemian settlers, though even here the population was predominantly English. The "melting pot" had begun to boil. These various strains were beginning to merge into a distinctive national type that was already recognizable in the mid-eighteenth century, and the word "American" was commonly used on both sides of the Atlantic to describe the people of the thirteen colonies.

Whereas the first great immigration to America was primarily English, beginning in the mid-eighteenth century successive waves of immigrants arrived from Scotland and Northern Ireland. These were called Scotch-Irish and they came to the New World as the result of a series of political upheavals in the Old. In Scotland a revolt against English rule had failed when the Jacobite armies of Scotch highlanders, led by Prince Charles Edward, were defeated by the English Lord Cumberland at Culloden, near Inverness. In Ireland a harsh land bill introduced by the English drove many small Irish farmers off the land.

They came to America in a migration that was to

be repeated again and again. America provided a haven, a safety valve for the tensions and pressures generated by the inequities of the European societies. Each political upheaval, each natural calamity in Europe, generated a new wave of immigration to America.

The Scotch-Irish came toward the end of the eighteenth century. They came after most of the good land along the Atlantic tidal plains had already been divided among the aristocratic families that comprised a New World landed gentry. So they pushed west, beyond the coastal plains, and settled in the mountain range that stretches from Pennsylvania, south into Georgia. They carved small farms out of the forested valleys and the sides of rocky hills. They farmed, hunted, cut timber, mined coal, and distilled a potent whiskey.

They brought with them a fundamentalist, Presbyterian religion and a fierce commitment to freedom. They also brought a remarkably rich and varied musical tradition. Theirs was a music of sturdy hymns, sung solemnly in simple and stately melody. Theirs was also a music of ballads, of lovely lilting song that told stories of love, tragic heroes, of everyday work and problems. It was a music of wild fiddle reels and foot-thumping highland jigs. Its instruments were the dulcimer and guitar, the fiddle and the bagpipe, the lute, and later the banjo.

When this music moved west and north along with the course of history, it changed. In the North, a Scandinavian and French strain was added and it be-

Appalachian music grew from a rich heritage that included sturdy hymns, soft ballads, and wild fiddle reels.

came the song of the lumberjacks, or shanty boys as they were also called. The word itself came from the French *chanter*—to sing—and song was the indispensable accompaniment to the rhythm of the ax.

The Elizabethan ballad, brought to America by the Scotch-Irish, was modified in structure and form to serve a new purpose here in the great pine and fir forests. It became a vehicle for expressing the life of these hard-working pioneers. The songs of the shanty-boys dealt with the experiences of everyday life, reflecting the values and the aspirations of the people who sang them.

"A Shantyman's Life" celebrated the rigors of daily routine in vigorous melody sung to a sprightly rhythm. "The Little Brown Bulls" told of his work on the river, hauling the huge log rafts to the sawmills.

"The Logger's Boast" reflected the shantyboy's pride in his work and celebrated his physical prowess. "The Jam on Gerry's Rock" described, in a doleful dirge, a log jam and the death of a lumberjack.

The opening of the West brought another adaptation of the Elizabethan ballad. Here the English strain was mixed with Spanish music, which merged in a musical form that expressed the peculiar conditions of western life. These conditions gave birth to the cowboy and his distinctive musical style.

A simple person, close to the fundamentals of living and working, the cowboy sang songs that were simple in design and structure with a touch of the monotonous rhythm of a trotting horse in their expression. The guitar was the principal instrument of the West and its melodically percussive chords shaped the harmonies of western music.

In his work the cowboy was a lonely man and his songs overflowed with nostalgic sentiments for home, a girl, peace. His best friend was his horse and his greatest fear was an unmarked grave somewhere on the endless prairie. He sang about both, lamenting his lonely life and his fear of dying alone. He also sang about cutting up and breaking loose in Abilene or Dodge City at the end of a long cattle drive.

Some of the Scotch-Irish went to sea where the ballad became the *chantey*—the sailor's song—another word deriving from the French *chanter*. Here again, music played an indispensable role, for the sailor needed song as much as he needed food and fresh water to see him through the long days at sea.

But chanteys were more than mere songs. They were a vital part of the everyday life of the sailor. Chanteys fall into four rough categories, each derived from a specific type of work it was designed to accompany. Songs sung to tasks calling for short, heavy pulls such as reefing and shortening sails were called "short drags." They had abrupt rhythms and crisp accents as in "Haul Away, Joe" and "Haul in the Bowline."

Songs that accompanied more sustained or heavier jobs, such as hoisting sail or weighing anchor, were called "halliards" and were sung in a typical "call and response" pattern to a steady, fairly vigorous rhythm. A solo voice would sing a lead melody which the remainder of the group would answer in a rich harmony.

For still more monotonous jobs there were "capstans" with long sustained melodies and slow, marchlike rhythms. Capstans were sung while loading or unloading cargo, or while rowing the longboats between ship and shore.

Finally, there were "foc'sle songs." These were not work songs like the chanteys, but songs meant purely for entertainment and relaxation when the crew was off duty. Like the cowboy and lumberjack songs these reflected the everyday life and interests of the sailors. They sang about strange ports and people, about ladies they left behind and those they would meet, epics of whaling and fishing, ballads celebrating the feats of great sea heroes. Because the crews of early American sailing ships were made up of sailors from all over the world, the chantey became a fertile meet-

ing ground for various national musical styles and forms. In the American sea chantey, we can trace a number of musical influences that range from Portuguese to sibilant Polynesian songs, from the English hornpipe to the Norwegian sailor's dance.

In this way the English ballad, the roots of which go back to the troubadour tradition of medieval Europe, was reshaped and transformed. The form was modified by other musical traditions as well as different conditions of life in the New World, and was—along with Puritan psalms and hymns and an African tradition brought by slaves—one of the fundamental building blocks of an indigenous American music.

In the Appalachian highlands, however, the Scotch-Irish ballad was preserved in a pure form down into the twentieth century. The settlers who pushed into the Appalachian chain at the end of the eighteenth century became isolated. History passed them by. A growing nation sprawled over the mountains and spread onto the plains. Cut off by inaccessible hills and valleys, the proud and aloof mountain people built a society in isolation from the rest of the country. It drew upon a fundamentalist, fire and brimstone religion and retained the manners and speech of eighteenth-century Scotland and Ireland. It evolved around family clans and small mountain farms.

Here musicologists, who, at the beginning of the twentieth century were seeking the roots of American music, discovered a tradition that retained many of the features of Elizabethan England. They heard and later recorded madrigals and ballads like "Barbara

Allen" and "Green Sleeves" that were unchanged since the eighteenth century settlers first brought them to the Appalachian highlands.

In 1904 Emma Bell Miles, a musicologist who made a study of Appalachian music, described her findings in an article titled "Some Real American Music," which appeared in *Harper's Magazine*. She called this a peculiarly American expression, a music that would repay serious study.

But outside of a few scholars and musicologists who concerned themselves with this *subculture,* little was heard of this music by the rest of the country for the next twenty years. Then the twentieth century encroached upon the hills and valleys of Appalachia. Roads were torn through the valleys. Railroads carried the produce of farm and mine, along with the people, into the rest of the country. Two wars called the men down from the hills to fight in distant worlds. Finally, radio came and the mountain people were no longer isolated.

The study of this music provided a fascinating insight into the development and propagation of folk music. Here were songs in their original form, which had undergone profound changes as they moved across the land. Thus an old Irish ballad, preserved in Appalachia, "The Old Man Rocking the Cradle," with the lines "Ay ay ay, my darling lie easy, / It's my misfortune and none of your own," becomes the familiar cowboy song with the lines "Whoopie tie yie yo, get along little dogie / It's your misfortune and none of my own."

The English madrigal, a song form dating back to the Middle Ages, was brought to Appalachia in the eighteenth century. Madrigals and ballads flourished, changed, and became part of the body of American folk song.

An English ballad about a young soldier dying of a venereal disease is transformed into the familiar cowboy lament, "As I Walked Down the Streets of Laredo." In this version the cowboy, though dying of a gun shot wound, retains many of the symptoms of the soldier, and is also "wrapped in white linen," and, completely out of character for a cowboy, requests a military funeral with fifes and drums.

An Irish ballad about an American utopia, "Canada Iho," becomes first a song about lumberjacks in the Northwest, and then a remarkably detailed and accurate ballad describing the experience of a gang of buffalo skinners.

Central to American folk song, then, was the ballad brought to America by Scotch-Irish settlers in the mid-eighteenth century. This tradition was enriched and modified in the New World by the addition of many different national strains and the peculiar conditions of American life. Here the ballad flourished with a variety and strength that was expressive of a young, diversified, and rapidly changing culture. Ranging from lilting songs with delicate melodies to coarse and bawdy ballads, from old songs carefully preserved to senseless scraps and bits of forgotten songs lumped together into a new expression, the remarkably rich body of American folk song grew and developed.

7. THE JIM CROW SHOW

AN IMPORTANT FEATURE of southern plantation life was the "Jubilee," a slave celebration that usually accompanied the periodic distribution of clothes, special prizes, and favors. All the people of the plantation participated on these occasions, and over the years a distinctive pageant of music, dance, and comedy developed to celebrate the Jubilee.

We cannot say for certain when the custom began, but we do know that it was already well established in the colonial period. Shepard N. Edmonds, a Negro born in Tennessee of freed-slave parents, gives us this description which he heard from his parents:

> It was generally on Sundays, when there was little work, that the slaves both young and old would dress up in hand-me-down finery to do a high-kicking, prancing walk-around. They did a take-off on the high manners of the white folks in the "big

house," but their masters gathered around to watch
the fun, missed the point. It's supposed to be that
the custom of a prize started with the master giving
a cake to the couple that did the proudest, most
original movement. . . .

The Jubilee was, basically, an entertainment that
allowed expression of the musical and comic talents
of the Negroes. As such it was an important factor in
plantation life. Most of the plantations that supported
a slave population were large, many of them encompassing thousands of acres. These stately plantations
were like kingdoms, isolated from one another by vast
distances and inadequate transportation facilities.

Consequently, each plantation was a self-sufficient
economic unit. In the early period everything needed
for life—food, clothing, building materials, tools—
was produced by the plantation. Later, as the plantations grew more wealthy, luxuries and fineries were
imported to grace the stately manor houses that provided the nucleus of the plantation.

But it was the land that determined the basic pulse
and rhythm of plantation life. All wealth was in the
land, and the rotation of crops, the planting and reap-
ing, the tilling of the soil, were the central drama
around which life revolved. Ulrich B. Phillips in his
Life and Labor in the Old South, described this existence:

> The plantation was pageant and variety show in al-
> ternation. The procession of plowmen at evening,
> slouched crosswise on their mules; the dance in the
> new sugarhouse, preceded by prayer; the bonfire in

the quarter with contests in clogs, cakewalks and charlestons whose fascinations were as yet undiscovered by the great world; the work songs in solo and refrain, with not too fast a rhythm; the baptizing in the creek, with lively demonstrations from the "sisters" as they came dripping out; the torchlight pursuit of 'possum and 'coon, with full-voiced halloo to baying houn' dog and yelping cur; the rabbit hunt, the log-rolling, the house-raising, the husking-bee, the children's play, all punctuated plantation life—and most of them were highly vocal. A funeral now and then of some prominent slave would bring festive sorrowing or the death of a beloved master an outburst of emotion. . . .

The rhythm of plantation life was also modified by visits that, because they were rare, were always an important social event. The visitor might have been from a neighboring plantation or a relative just arrived by ship from England. In all cases a visit was an event that provided a welcome change from the everyday pace of life.

Gentlemen amateurs would bring out their hautboys, French horns, violins, flutes, and harpsichords to perform the classic works of European masters. A stately minuet may have been danced in the salon to celebrate the occasion, and the more daring may have introduced the "racy" waltz. If the visitor came from abroad he might have brought some new music which would be enthusiastically performed.

But then, after the genteel entertainment had been finished, the party would move out to the lawn where the slaves would perform a show of their own. Here

After the genteel entertainment in the ballroom of the "big house," the party would move outdoors where the slaves would perform.

was a different music and a different approach to singing and dancing, which was looked upon by the people of the "big house" with tolerant amusement. It was all very "primitive" and "childish," yet the infectious rhythms, the songs, the high-stepping dances and walk-arounds of the Negro field hands exerted an irresistible fascination and the Jubilee was a featured part of all important social occasions.

So effective was this celebration in terms of entertainment that it was soon copied on the stage. Oddly enough, the first accounts we have of professional performances of this kind come to us from England. Perhaps an Englishman connected with the theatre saw a Jubilee and recognized its potential for the stage. However it came about, there began to appear in Eng-

lish music halls during the last decades of the eighteenth century acts in which Negro impersonations were featured. In these performances white entertainers darkened their faces with burnt cork and proceeded to sing in an exaggerated Negro dialect and dance to tunes they described as "plantation melodies."

In America, as far as we know, blackface entertainment by white performers did not begin until the second decade of the nineteenth century. During that period this type of theatrical fare became increasingly popular and performers like George Washington Dixon, and "Daddy" Rice were laying the foundations for what was to become the minstrel show—a wholly unique and novel theatrical form that was completely a product of the American scene and experience.

Both Dixon and Rice performed in music halls, singing and dancing in blackface to the accompaniment of banjo and bones—two flattened bones or sticks held in the fingers of the closed fist and snapped together with a rolling motion of the wrist to produce remarkably varied percussive effects. At first their acts consisted of nothing more than a series of songs and dances that aped the music and movements of plantation Negroes. Over the years these individual acts merged into an integrated theatrical form of immense vitality which captured the imagination of the American public.

The prototype for the classic minstrel show, which was to have such a marked influence upon American popular music, made its debut in New York City in 1843 when a troupe opened in February of that year, at the Bowery Amphitheatre, in an entertainment promoted as "the novel, grotesque, and surpassingly melodious Ethiopian Band, entitled, Virginia Minstrels." The advertisements went on to say that this was "an exclusively minstrel entertainment, entirely exempt from the vulgarities and other objectionable features which have hitherto characterized Negro extravaganzas."

"Negro extravaganzas," then, were a familiar form of theatrical entertainment, and this troupe was apparently organized to exploit a form that was already popular. The cast was made up of four performers, all of whom had theatrical experience: Daniel Decatur Emmett, who played the violin and was to achieve a degree of immortality with his composition of "Dixie"; Billy Whitlock, banjo; Frank Bower, bones; and Richard Pelham, tambourine.

Dressed in exaggerated costumes, wearing white trousers, calico shirts, and long swallow-tailed jackets, their faces blackened with burnt cork, the Virginia Minstrels made their debut. On stage they proceeded to entertain a delighted audience with a shrewd combination of singing, dancing, Negro dialect patter, and instrumental music.

The novel feature of the Virginia Minstrels was this association of four entertainers performing as a coordinated team, each playing a characteristic instrument and comic role, and putting on a complete, self-contained show. Four-man teams became the standard cast of the typical minstrel show which sprang to immense popularity in the two decades preceding the Civil War.

Three years later, in 1847, a second minstrel show organized by Edwin P. Christy and called *Christy's Minstrels* opened at Palmo's Opera House in New York City. So successful was this production that Christy leased Mechanic's Hall on Broadway the next year where his troupe played for the next ten years. Christy also claimed to have organized the first true minstrel show in Buffalo in 1842.

Although the origins of the minstrel show are vague, these two troupes undoubtedly established the pattern that was to dominate the minstrel throughout the nineteenth century. The performance was divided into two acts. In the first act the performers were ar-

A nineteenth-century poster announcing Christy's Minstrels.

ranged in a semicircle on the stage. The "Interlocutor," a kind of straight man, was seated in the center. The Interlocutor generally played in whiteface and wore full-dress clothes. Seated at either end of the semicircle were the endmen, "Mr. Tambo," who played the tambourine, and "Mr. Bones," who played bones.

The program opened with a chorus as the performers made a grand entrance, marching around the stage in imitation of the plantation cakewalk. At the conclusion of the march the Interlocutor gave the stereotyped command, "Gentlemen, be seated."

Then followed a series of jokes between the Interlocutor and the endmen, interspersed with ballads, comic songs, and instrumental numbers played chiefly on violin and banjo. In this opening act each member of the company was given the opportunity to display his talents in song, dance, and comedy.

The second act was called the "olio" and consisted of a series of individual routines, a farce, burlesque opera, and more dialect jokes. The grand finale was a singing and dancing number called the "walk-around" in which the entire company participated, each member doing a specialty, in turn, while the others sang and clapped hands.

Although modified and altered by different companies, this was the classic form of the minstrel show as it was performed on the American stage. After 1870 the shows became more lavish and spectacular, and in the 1880's it was not unusual to have as many as one hundred performers in a troupe. These productions were called "gigantean," "mammoth," "gargantuan," and "extravaganzas."

By 1850 there were some seventy-five companies performing minstrel shows in theatres all over America, and troupes toured England, Europe, and South America. In 1860 the number of troupes had doubled. Then, after 1870, the popularity of the minstrel show began to wane. It practically disappeared as a theatrical form by the beginning of the twentieth century, though it remained an influence in popular entertainment. Al Jolson, for example, appeared in blackface in the 1920's and early 1930's.

Blackface minstrels dominated the American musical theatre for almost seventy years. During this period it brought to birth and kept alive a vast body of American popular music the vitality and exuberance of which were recognized by all who heard it, and which exerted a strong influence on subsequent musical development in America.

Musically, the minstrel was a typical American mélange of sources and folk traditions. The basic influence was undoubtedly that of the southern Negro, but this tradition was altered and modified on the stage by performers who were mostly white. In this music, then, we can trace a derivation that could have occurred only in America. This music, the popularity of which swept the nation, was an Anglo-American modification of an Afro-American modification of English, Scotch, Irish, German, French, and Spanish originals.

At its best, minstrel music was full of vitality and exuberance on the one hand, and poignant sentimentality on the other. Many of its songs have withstood the test of time and are still heard and sung today. Probably the most influential of the minstrel composers were Daniel Decatur "Ol Dan" Emmett and Stephen Collins Foster. Songs by both have achieved the status of national folk music.

"Ol' Dan" Emmett was born in Mt. Vernon, Ohio, October 29, 1815, to an Irish-American pioneer family. The first of four children, Daniel received little formal schooling though he learned to read and write while helping in his father's smithy. At thirteen he was apprenticed to a printer, but never followed this trade. Always attracted to music, he learned to play the fife and drum and joined the Army as a fifer-drummer when he was seventeen.

After his discharge from the army in 1835 Emmett joined the Spalding and Rogers' Circus as a drummer with the band. With the circus Emmett traveled all over America, and during this period he also learned to play the violin and flute. Army and circus bands provided the major portion of Emmett's musical training though he had always been musical.

"As far back as I can remember," Emmett told an interviewer in his later years, "I took great interest in music. I hummed familiar tunes, arranged words to sing to them, and made up tunes to suit words of my own. I paid no especial attention to poetry and thought little about the literary merit of what I wrote. I composed *Old Dan Tucker* when I was fifteen or sixteen years old, before I left Mt. Vernon."

In this case, composition meant simply putting words to an already familiar tune. Indeed, several theatrical figures of the time claimed the composition of this song. For example, an English music hall singer who came to America in 1831, Henry Russel, claimed he composed the tune accidentally in Rochester, New York, in 1835, by playing a familiar hymn twice as fast as it was regularly performed.

Modern musicologists trace the syncopated, sprightly musical treatment of the melody of "Old Dan Tucker" to an Afro-American modification of a Protestant hymn. This kind of disputation was typical of the early years of minstrelsy and offers us an insight into how the repertoire of this theatrical form grew.

A manuscript of "Dixie," autographed by its composer, Daniel Decatur Emmett.

Performers picked up likely material wherever they heard it, modified melody and lyrics, and used it in their acts, more often than not claiming both as original.

Emmett's most popular song was unquestionably

composed by him. "Dixie," which was first performed on April 4, 1859, was written as a "walk-around" for Bryant's Minstrels with whom Emmett was associated during his most creative period, 1858 to 1868.

During this period Emmett composed upwards of 300 songs, including some forty "walk-arounds." Many of these songs, especially the "walk-arounds" were extremely popular and would have ranked high in the popularity charts of his day. Some, like "Dixie," "Turkey In The Straw," "Old Time Rocks," and "Road to Georgia," have become standards of American popular musical expression.

"Dixie," though it was composed in New York City by a songwriter born in Ohio, became the unofficial anthem of the Confederate South during the Civil War. It was played at the inauguration of Confederate President, Jefferson Davis, and many southern regiments used it as their marching song. Emmett, whose sympathies were wholly with the Union, is reported as having said, "If I had known to what use they were going to put my song, I'll be damned if I'd have written it."

At the end of the Civil War, President Lincoln, displaying a characteristic humor and humanity, restored "Dixie" to the Union. A crowd had assembled outside the White House the day after Lee surrendered, to serenade the President with a band. Lincoln made a brief speech and then asked the band to play "Dixie." "I had heard that our adversaries over the way had attempted to appropriate it. I insisted yesterday that we had fairly captured it. . . . I presented the question

93

to the Attorney General, and he gave his opinion that it is our lawful prize. I ask the band to give us a good turn on it. . . ."

Emmett retired from the theatre in 1888 to a small country home near his native town of Mt. Vernon. He made one more theatrical appearance with Field's Minstrels, in a triumphant tour in 1895. He made his final appearance on April 11, 1896, and returned to his home in Ohio where he lived until his death on June 28, 1904, at the age of eighty-eight.

Stephen Foster, though he achieved popularity that rivaled that of Emmett, did not fare as well. Born at Lawrenceville, Pennsylvania, later a part of Pittsburgh, on July 4, 1826, Foster was to leave an indelible imprint upon American music. Although his family was reasonably well-off, Stephen had no settled career and no formal musical training. Always drawn to music, he began composing songs as a boy.

Encouraged by the success of "Oh, Susanna," written in 1848, Foster decided to devote himself to music. The song brought him to the attention of Edwin P. Christy, and Foster was commissioned to write songs in the "Ethiopian" manner for the minstrel. The most famous of these songs were "Camptown Races" (1850), "Old Folks at Home" (1851), "My Old Kentucky Home" (1852), "Old Black Joe" (1860), and "Oh, Susanna."

Foster's attitude toward these songs, upon which his reputation rests, was ambivalent. It reflected the attitude of the society as a whole. Foster was brought up in genteel respectability and the respectable world looked down their noses at the minstrel show. It was considered vulgar, crass, and common, a theatrical form with which no self-respecting person would be associated.

This attitude was reflected in Foster's own mind. Though his "Ethiopian" songs were immensely popular Foster never whole-heartedly accepted them himself. He refused to allow his name to be associated with his early minstrel songs because he feared the association would hurt his reputation as a composer of "refined" music. Later he changed his mind and wrote Edwin P. Christy in a letter dated May, 1852, that he had decided to "pursue the Ethiopian business without fear or shame," and asked that his name appear on publications of his music.

A year later Foster was assuring the editor of *The Musical World and Times* of New York that he would henceforth devote his talents to the composition of "white men's music." One part of Stephen Foster aspired to the composition of sentimental ballads and elegant songs, to be sung by equally sentimental and elegant young ladies in the best society. The other part of Stephen Foster was uncannily sympathetic to the tenor of his times, reflecting the sentiments and vitality of a vigorous young nation.

These two extremes were never reconciled, and in his last years the "genteel" aspect of his nature appears to have become dominant. He wrote his last "plantation" melodies in 1860 and thereafter devoted his time to the composition of "refined" songs. Between 1860 and his death in 1863 Foster wrote more

"Daddy" Rice performing the minstrel song "Jim Crow," a title that later became an epithet signifying discrimination against Negroes and a hostile way of describing them.

than one hundred songs, only one of which has survived the test of time. This was "Beautiful Dreamer, Wake Unto Me," which was composed in 1863.

Stephen Foster died alone on the afternoon of January 13, 1864—barely thirty-eight years old—in a paupers' ward at New York City's Bellevue Hospital. His last years were marked by a disastrous physical and moral degeneration. Before he died, America's greatest songwriter had degenerated into an alcoholic hack who tried to fit his talents into a mold prescribed by a "genteel" society. The mold, apparently, was too much for the talent.

Emmett and Foster parallel the meteoric career of American minstrelsy. Both were swept up in the creative vortex of this indigenous form and both made

96

significant contributions to a developing American music. Both reflect the weakness and strength of the minstrel.

In one sense, the "Ethiopian business" was a tragic development. The classic minstrel show was nothing more than another example of the exploitation of the Negro by white men. It borrowed freely from a musical idiom that reflected a true Negro musical genius, while it degraded the originators. The conventionalized form of the minstrel, with its interlocutor and two stooges with tambourine and bones, crystallized the white myth of the grinning, toothy, lazy, good-for-nothing, yet innocently happy "darky." In fact the title of an early minstrel song became descriptive of the social and economic oppression of the Negro, "Jim Crow."

Musically, however, the minstrel show provided an important chapter in the development of a true American music. In its search for popular material the minstrel drew on every musical resource of the New World. It mixed Scotch-Irish ballads and reels with Protestant hymns, Negro spirituals with German folk melodies, the French Quadrille with the jig, Mississippi work songs with English music hall ballads, in a mélange that expressed a distinctively American voice.

8. THE GENTEEL TRADITION AND THE GREAT SPLIT

THE NINETEENTH CENTURY was a period of spectacular growth and development. When it began, America was a loose federation of thirteen newly independent colonies struggling for national existence. Its territory was limited to the Atlantic Seaboard. Beyond was wilderness whose ownership was contested by a number of European powers.

Then, in an unparalleled expansion, the young nation grew. It swept over the Appalachian highlands and spilled onto the plains. Manifest destiny carried the new nation to the shores of the Pacific. America survived a brutal and bloody civil war and emerged into the twentieth century a world power.

In one respect America's music kept pace with this dramatic growth. The nineteenth century saw a distinctive music take form and flourish. A mixture of musical traditions from practically the entire world, this music added the shape and cadence of the vast spaces and optimism of a growing nation. It found its first expression in a popular voice the eclectic exuberance and vitality of which gave it a distinct character to which all the peoples of the world could respond.

In another respect music lagged pathetically behind national development. American popular expression, which was to have such a marked influence upon twentieth-century music, was dismissed as of little consequence by an influential portion of the population. The polarity of American music into hostile factions, evident in the earliest colonial period, became even more pronounced, reaching a peak in the late 1800's.

Throughout the nineteenth century, American music was a house divided. On one side was a lusty, earthy, vigorous folk music that gave voice to the popular spirit and aspirations of a new nation. On the other, there was "art" music which derived from a snobbish, emasculated, precious gentility which looked to the Old World for its model and inspiration.

Although this division had little apparent effect upon the surging development of popular music, its effect upon American art music was disastrous. "Serious" musical creation in nineteenth-century America was negligible at best. Eliminate it and nothing vital is lost in the cultural continuity of America.

We cannot even point to a dearth of composers during this period to explain this hundred-year blank. Throughout the nineteenth century American cities

George Caleb Bingham captured the spirit of lusty folk music in his painting "Jolly Flatboatmen" of 1857.

and schools supported a sizable population of professional musicians and composers. There was, in fact, a steady march of deadly serious composers bent upon revealing as much soul as they were capable of bringing to their creation. Unfortunately the music they produced, however noble in intent and technically proficient, proved to be little more than academic exercises in a European idiom that had nothing to do with the forces that were making America. Art music was being composed during this period, but it was an art music without roots, a music cut off from the mainstream of the American spirit by snobbism, at worst, and a misguided aestheticism, at best.

An unfortunate dualism haunted all aspects of American cultural life. Because this was a young nation, crude at times and boisterous, there was a corresponding tendency in the upper classes toward the cultivation of gentility. This preoccupation was reflected in magazines and periodicals of the time, which devoted an inordinate amount of space to guides and manuals that advised readers as to "proper and refined social deportment." Mark Twain wrote a brilliant, scathing satire on this kind of social manual.

In their obsession with good taste, manners, refinement, cultivated Americans sought to imitate or import the trappings of European culture, and American art composers of the time were cultivated, if nothing else. While folk and popular music (which also had roots in the Old World) were being gradually transformed by the American experience, art music developed for a century with scarcely any organic relationship to its immediate environment. It was a hothouse flower growing in an inaccessible ivory tower.

As a result the massive manuscripts of an endless stream of "grand" symphonies, operas, oratorios, symphonic fantasies, concertos, and symphony concertantes composed during this period have moldered on obscure library shelves. Here they remain, unheard and forgotten. The dust that settles on their jackets is disturbed only on the rare occasion when some research student produces a doctoral dissertation. Against all this earnest endeavor only a pitifully small handful of musical innovators kept alive a spark of original creativity.

Typical of the forgotten nineteenth-century American composer was George Frederick Bristow. He was born in Brooklyn, New York, on December 19, 1825, and died in 1898, his life having spanned almost three-quarters of the century. Bristow is interesting today mainly because he is the first American art composer who received all of his musical education in the New World.

Like so many musical figures Bristow revealed his aptitude early. As a boy he studied the violin, and is reputed to have begun playing professionally at the age of eleven in the orchestra of the Olympic Theatre in New York. He later studied theory and harmony with Henry Christian Timm, a native of Hamburg, Germany. Timm came to New York in 1835 where he soon established himself as an influential figure in the musical life of the city. He was a popular teacher, soloist, and one of the founders of the New York Philharmonic Society in 1842, and its president from 1847 to 1864.

Bristow was one of the original members of the Philharmonic Society Orchestra and its conductor from 1851 to 1862. In all, he spent some forty years with the orchestra both as violinist and conductor. As a composer, Bristow was more prolific than original, but he was one of the first Americans to deal successfully with the traditional forms of European art music. Included in his creative output were a number of symphonies and one opera.

Although none of his works has survived the test of time Bristow's industry and competence earned him a reputation as a professional composer. He was successful in his lifetime and his works were performed regularly over a period of some fifty years. His symphonies were played by orchestras all over America and his oratorios and chamber music enjoyed considerable vogue. The overture to his opera, *Columbus,* was first performed by the New York Philharmonic Society in the first concert given by the orchestra in Steinway Hall on 14th Street, November 17, 1866.

More typical of the American composer of this period was William Mason (1829–1908), son of Doctor Lowell Mason of Boston, an influential music publisher. Mason is more typical because, unlike Bristow, he received his musical training abroad. After preliminary study with Henry Schmidt in Boston young Mason made what was to become a required pilgrimage for all Americans seriously interested in music— he went to Europe. And going to Europe, for an American musical scholar of the time, meant going to Germany.

In Germany Mason enrolled at the conservatory in Leipzig where he studied theory and composition with Moscheles and Hauptmann. Later he studied with Franz Liszt at Weimar. One of his first compositions, a salon piece for piano titled "Les Perles de

Rosée," was dedicated to Liszt. Mason spent a total of five years absorbing Teutonic culture before returning to America to spread the gospel of "good" music.

He settled in Boston where he became a successful piano teacher and a leader of the city's musical circles. He organized a string quartet with which he appeared as pianist in chamber concerts, and he also toured as a piano soloist. William Mason's family history is worth mentioning because of its musical tradition. His great-grandfather, Barachias Mason, conducted a singing school in Boston. Johnson Mason, his grandfather, a civic-minded banker, found time in his busy schedule to play the cello and sing in the parish choir. His father, Lowell Mason, passed from the family banking business to a full-time, lucrative career as a music publisher, beginning this venture with a book of hymns for which he provided a "modern" harmonic notation. William Mason followed the tradition and established a respected career, the culmination of four generations of New England musical endeavor.

William Mason also helped establish the precedent for musical study in Germany. Following in his footsteps, a steady stream of American musical lights crossed the sea to absorb the mystic-Teutonic aura of the land of Bach, Beethoven, and Brahms. John Knowles Paine of Portland, Maine, another influential nineteenth-century American composer, made the trek to Berlin in 1857, before he was appointed di-

The Mendelssohn Quintette Club of Boston, one of many musical groups that flourished in the 1800's.

rector of music at Harvard College. Paine went on to write three symphonies, a number of oratorios, and shorter choral works, as well as songs, several symphonic poems, and an opera. These works were performed regularly during his lifetime and were received with respectful enthusiasm by his musical colleagues.

Frederic Grant Gleason (1848–1903), Dudley Buck (1839–1909), and Silas Gamaliel Pratt (1846–1916) were three more American composers of the period who made the German pilgrimage in their student days in order to bring a sample of Old World culture back to their raw and unlettered countrymen.

All three were respected composers and teachers in their time. Their works were regularly performed not only in America, but in Europe as well. All three have been passed over in the wake of history, their music forgotten for the most part, and their memories little more than footnotes in the history of American music.

Probably the most influential of America's Teutonic composers was Edward Alexander MacDowell (1861–1908), virtually the only nineteenth-century composer whose works are still occasionally performed. In many ways MacDowell marked the high point of the genteel tradition in American music, encompassing in his person all the strength and weakness of the school.

Edward MacDowell was born in New York City on December 18, 1861. His father, of Scotch-Irish descent, was a prosperous businessman, while his mother espoused the cultural and artistic pretensions of upper-class New York society. Although there is no record of a musical heritage in the family, Edward exhibited his musical gifts early and began studying the piano with a family friend when he was eight years old.

He proved to be an apt pupil and was soon taken to a professional teacher, Paul Desvernine with whom he studied until he was fifteen. Determined to pursue a career in music, Edward felt the need to go abroad to continue his studies. Accompanied by his mother, he embarked on a European sojourn that was to last for the next twelve years.

Edward first studied at the Paris Conservatory where the methods and atmosphere appeared to have been uncongenial for the young American. Leaving Paris, MacDowell and his mother first went to Stuttgart, then Wiesbaden, and finally settled at the Frankfort Conservatory. Here young MacDowell came under the influence of Joachim Raff, director of the conservatory, who became something of a spiritual mentor to the American.

It was Raff who encouraged MacDowell to cultivate his gift for composition. After completing his studies, MacDowell accepted the position of principal piano teacher at the nearby Darmstadt Conservatory. He held this position for one year during which he commuted between Frankfort and Darmstadt while continuing his association with Raff. This proved to be a fruitful and creative period for MacDowell. He taught, performed as piano soloist, and applied himself increasingly to composition.

In 1882 MacDowell visited Franz Liszt at Weimar. He showed the manuscript of his First Piano Concerto to the Hungarian virtuoso. Liszt was favorably impressed with the work and encouraged the young American. Later it was upon Liszt's recommendation that MacDowell's Second Modern Suite, Opus 14, was published by Breitkopf & Hartel in Leipzig.

In June 1884, MacDowell returned briefly to America where he married Marian Nevins, a pupil who had studied with him in Darmstadt. A few days after his marriage MacDowell returned to Europe with his wife. He settled in Wiesbaden in a small cottage where he continued teaching and composing. During this time MacDowell's reputation as a composer was steadily growing. His orchestral and instrumental works were being performed in Europe and America. A number of American musicians began coming to Wiesbaden to visit the composer and his wife. They urged him to return to America.

Finally, in September, 1888, MacDowell and his wife sailed for the United States. The couple settled in Boston, which, at the time, was something of a German musical province. He remained in Boston for eight years, except for a brief trip to Europe in the summer of 1889. He appeared as a soloist, playing his Second Piano Concerto at a concert of American music organized and conducted by Frank Van der Stucken in Paris, July 12, 1889. This ambitious program included the works of Dudley Buck, George Chadwick, Arthur Foote, Henry Huss, Margaret Lang, John Paine, and Frank Van der Stucken.

MacDowell joined the faculty of Columbia University in New York when that institution established a professorship of music in 1896. Although he was a popular and enthusiastic teacher, he differed with the school board on matters of policy. As a result of these differences MacDowell resigned from the university in 1904 in what was to become a *cause célèbre*. As a consequence of the publicity that followed his resignation, MacDowell suffered a nervous collapse

Edward Alexander MacDowell is virtually the only nineteenth-century American composer of serious music whose works are still performed.

from which he never recovered. He died in New York City on January 23, 1908.

Three years before his death Lawrence Gilman summed up the position of MacDowell in American music, in his essay on the composer in *Living Masters of Music*:

> He was one of the most individual writers who ever made music—as individual as Chopin, or Debussy, or Brahms, or Grieg. . . . Vitality—an abounding freshness, a perpetual youthfulness—was one of his prime traits; nobility—nobility of style and impulse —was another. The morning freshness, the welling spontaneity of his music, even in moments of ex-

alted or passionate utterance, was continually surprising: it was music not unworthy of the golden ages of the world.

Twenty years later another critic, Paul Rosenfeld, appraised his work more realistically:

> The music of Edward MacDowell amounts more to an assimilation of European motives, figures, and ideas than to an original expression. In any case, the original elements are small and of minor importance. . . .

MacDowell is remembered today principally for his small piano pieces such as "To a Wild Rose," "To a Water Lily," and his collection titled "Sea Pieces." His orchestral and choral works are rarely heard, sharing the neglect of his ambitious piano sonatas and concertos.

When Edward MacDowell dominated America's musical life he was hailed by many as "the great American composer" long awaited by the nation. Yet history has shown that MacDowell was not a great composer. At best he was a talented miniaturist, composing a number of exquisite salon pieces for the piano. Creatively he belonged to the past rather than the future. He represented the decline of a tradition that had dominated American music throughout the nineteenth century. After the death of MacDowell the tradition began to fade in the face of the triumphal ascendancy of the popular spirit in American music.

The genteel tradition, however, was not completely

unfruitful. Although it did not produce anything of lasting musical value, it did encourage and stimulate an interest in music among the American people. In its wake came an entire musical superstructure that included symphony orchestras, opera companies, and music schools. During the nineteenth century the genteel tradition, with its obsessive concern for culture and refinement, spread across the continent. Musical societies flourished in every town or city prosperous enough to support such an establishment.

Important European soloists and composers came to America in response to this genuine concern, and the American musical public was thus intimately connected with Old World developments. Without this interest and support, the next great stage in the development of American music—the merging of art with the popular spirit—might never have occurred.

9. THE RUDE AWAKENING

IN NOVEMBER 1893, the New York Philharmonic Society presented a gala concert that attracted the attention of the entire American musical establishment. Featured on the program was the world première of a work by the world famous Bohemian composer, Anton Dvořák—his Symphony No. 5, titled *From The New World*. Advance publicity had described the composition as Dvořák's musical impression of America. Everyone in music wanted to hear how an established European composer would interpret the New World.

To understand the excitement generated by this première we must examine the state of American music at the time. As we have already seen, art music in America was dominated by a genteel tradition that looked to post-romantic Germany for inspiration. American music, as it was developing on the popular stage and in a growing body of folk expression, was ignored. It was dismissed from serious consideration as vulgar, crude, and cheap.

Our leading composers of the period looked upon music as a kind of ideal expression existing on an ethereal plane far removed from the vulgar concerns of everyday life. This credo was summed up by Edward MacDowell—the leading American musical light of the time—in one of his lectures at Columbia University:

> The high mission of music is neither to be an agent for expressing material things; nor to utter pretty sounds to amuse the ear; not a sensuous excitant to fire the blood, or a sedative to lull the senses; it is a language, but a language of the intangible, a soul language. . . .

No one can argue with the sentiments expressed by MacDowell. He was undoubtedly sincere in his views. Yet it was precisely this kind of idealism that cut music off from the mainstreams of American life, sequestering it in an ivory tower. It created a musical atmosphere that made it possible for its proponents to completely ignore developments that were occurring everywhere in the New World.

During the period when Dvořák was working on his symphony, the musical establishment knew little about, and cared less for, American native expression. As far as they were concerned it did not exist. This opinion was reflected by Louis C. Elson, a leading musicologist, when he wrote: "It must be admitted that in the field of folk music, America is rather barren."

113

A remarkable statement! Even more remarkable, this opinion was confirmed and concurred in by Frederic L. Ritter, another musicologist, in his study of American music, published in 1883, in which he asks rhetorically: "How are we to account for this utter absence of national people's music and poetry in America?"

It is difficult to imagine how such respected and influential scholars managed to overlook a music that was practically everywhere. Was it possible that they never heard a minstrel show or the sounds of a country barn dance? Or was it simply that they were so wrapped up in an aesthetic mystique that they never listened? Dvořák listened, and heard the land shaking with music.

More important, Dvořák used this music. Unawed by the genteel tradition, he wandered about the country with his ears open. He listened to the songs of Negro stevedores loading and unloading the steamboats that plied the Ohio and Mississippi rivers. He responded to the sprightly rhythms and the sentimental poignancy of minstrel songs. Negro spirituals, in particular, fascinated him, with their supple melodies and elegiac harmonies. Dvořák absorbed these sounds of America and utilized their spirit and originality in his compositions.

Perhaps the Bohemian composer's background explains his receptivity to native American music. Anton Dvořák was born in a small village near Prague on September 8, 1841. His father was an innkeeper and butcher of modest means. Dvořák was undoubtedly influenced by the amateur music-making which he heard and contributed to at the inn. He soon became an accomplished violinist and a perceptive local music teacher, A. Liehmann, recognizing his unusual talent, persuaded Dvořák's father to send him to the conservatory in Prague.

After two years of study Dvořák left the school to support himself as a professional musician. He played viola in an orchestra, the organ in a church, and taught, while writing his first serious compositions. His musical gifts were quickly recognized, and in 1875 Dvořák was awarded by the Austrian Government a state grant, which enabled him to devote more of his time to composition.

A superb melodic gift and the delightfully fresh Czech character of his music, together with superior technical equipment, quickly catapulted the young composer to world-wide acclaim. He was also fortunate to be working at a time when nationalism in music was encouraged.

It is not surprising that when Dvořák came to America at the height of his fame in 1892, he took an interest in the musical life around him. His work was rooted in the folk traditions of his native land. In America he deliberately sought out similar roots in order to absorb the spirit of this unfamiliar country.

Dvořák came to America in response to an invitation to be director of the National Conservatory of Music in New York City. This invitation was related to a pattern of cultural acquisition that had become significant in the latter part of the nineteenth century. The surging economic development of America had generated a large class of wealthy financiers, merchants, and industrialists. Like the *nouveau riche* everywhere, this class wanted visible evidence of their new status. They wanted the best, and the best at the time was in Europe.

Agents for American millionaires scoured Europe, stripping the Old World of art treasures, castles, furnishings—anything that could lend a measure of distinction to their New World palaces. Artists were drawn to America by the opportunities its wealth and enthusiasm offered.

Dvořák proved to be a most fortunate part of this cultural migration. Curious about America, the Bohemian traveled extensively and lived for a time in Spillville, Iowa. Everywhere he went, Dvořák listened to the music of the people. Unlike his American counterparts he did not limit his musical experience to the concert hall and salon. Instead he went to music halls and country dances. He heard the songs of farmers and Negro workers. The songs of Stephen Foster captivated him and Dvořák praised the American song-writer extravagantly. This at a time when Stephen Foster was considered little more than a commercial hack, when he was scarcely acknowledged at all by the musical establishment.

Dvořák became so enthusiastic about this country that he wrote a *Cantata to the American Flag* and even offered to compose a new anthem for the United States! Most of all Dvořák was drawn to the music of the Negro, which, at once exuberant and melancholy, reminded him so much of Slavic folk music.

The first notes of Dvořák's New World Symphony.

Henry Thacker Burleigh, a student of Dvořák's, described this responsiveness years later:

> Dvořák was deeply impressed by the old Negro "spirituals" and also by Stephen Foster's songs. It was my privilege to sing repeatedly some of the old plantation songs for him at his house, and one in particular, "Swing Low, Sweet Chariot," greatly pleased him. . . . He used to stop and ask if that was the way the slaves sang. . . .

This sensitivity to native expression was evident in his New World Symphony. The première caused a furor in American musical circles. Here was a work that breathed the spirit of a music that was despised by the genteel tradition. To make matters worse, its derivation was admitted frankly. Dvořák himself acknowledged it, before the première, in a statement in which he said the themes and spirit of his new

117

symphony were based on native musical themes, especially those sung by Negroes. He said:

> These beautiful and varied themes are the product of the soil. They are American. They are the folk songs of America and your composers must turn to them. In the Negro melodies of America I discover all that is needed for a great and noble school of music. . . .

Not so, answered the American Brahmins, led by the eminent Professor Edward MacDowell. Opposing Dvořák's suggestion, he rejected the concept of musical nationalism based upon folklore. In a scathing rebuttal to Dvořák, MacDowell wrote:

> We have here in America been offered a pattern for an American national musical costume by the Bohemian Dvořák—though what the Negro melodies have to do with Americanism in art still remains a mystery. . . . Masquerading in the so-called nationalism of Negro clothes cut in Bohemia will not help us. . . .

MacDowell's censure for all its vehemence, was too late. Historically it was little more than the last gasp of a dying tradition. For years before Dvořák's visit American music had been champing at the restrictions imposed by the genteel tradition and its Teutonic dominance. Rumblings of discontent were being sounded across the land. Dvořák's symphony and his suggestion that American composers "look homeward" came at an opportune moment. His sojourn in America, together with his creation of notable musical works inspired by his experiences in the New

World, symbolized a movement in American music that was beginning to take form at the time. Dvořák's presence merely accelerated the pace, the weight of his reputation lending respectability to the acceptance of American national music.

His influence, for example, was instrumental to the organization of the Wa-Wan Press in 1901, which was founded for the express purpose of publishing American music that would:

> . . . cease to see everything through German spectacles, however wonderful, however sublime those spectacles might be in themselves! . . . Thus fortified, we will no longer fear that the American composer is going to the dogs when he revels in a new and unusual combination of notes; that is, one which differs from the good old German tradition. . . .

Arthur Farwell, one of the founders of the press, had complained earlier that: "only German music sounds natural to concertgoers in the United States." The Wa-Wan Press, its manifesto went on to say, would do everything possible to: "launch a progressive movement in American music, including a definite acceptance of Dvořák's challenge to go after our own folk music."

Actually, the vitality of this country's native music had been recognized some fifty years earlier by one of the most remarkable figures in American music. Louis Moreau Gottschalk was the first world-acclaimed American virtuoso, and a composer of considerable talent as well. That his music was not more influential is a measure of the extent of the dominance of the genteel tradition upon American art music. Gottschalk's music derived frankly from native American folk music and as such was unacceptable to the musical establishment.

Louis Moreau Gottschalk was born in New Orleans on May 8, 1829. His father, Edward, a wealthy cotton broker, had come to New Orleans from England some ten years earlier. Here he met and married Aimée Marie de Brusle, whose grandfather had been governor of the French colony of Saint-Domingue. As a boy, Louis Moreau was brought up in the brilliant, colorful world of aristocratic New Orleans.

His musical debut was described years later by an elder sister: "One day, everyone in the family was startled by a faint, but most exquisite melody on the piano. When Mamma rushed into the drawing room, she found little Moreau standing tiptoe on a highstool, playing the melody she had sung to him in the morning. The tone and touch were perfect!" Louis Moreau was three years old at the time.

The family lost little time in arranging for a teacher. Louis studied violin and piano, but the piano always remained his favorite instrument. He gave his first public concert when he was eight years old, and, shortly before he was twelve, his father decided to send him to Europe for further study. Young Louis Moreau Gottschalk sailed for France in May 1842, after giving a farewell concert that was attended by all of New Orleans society.

In Paris Gottschalk was placed in a private school where he continued studying the piano and violin, while adding theory and composition to round out his musical education. Three years later, Gottschalk, only fifteen years old at the time, composed one of his most successful pieces. It was called "La Bamboula," and was written while he was convalescing from an illness. Perhaps the young American was homesick for New Orleans at the time, because this music was nothing more than an evocation of a Negro dance that he must have seen and heard as a boy. He composed two other piano pieces during this period, "La Savane," or "Ballad Creole," and "Le Bananier" (The Banana Tree) subtitled "Chanson Negre." All three reveal a nostalgia for home.

His Parisian sojourn, however, was far from trying. Through his family connections he was received and feted in the salons of the best French society, and his musical abilities were extravagantly appreciated.

He gave his first public concert at the Salle Pleyel in Paris, in April, 1845, just before his sixteenth birthday. He featured his three compositions on the program. The concert was a critical triumph for the young American and he found himself the center of admiring attention. Chopin, for example, saluted him as a future "king of pianists."

After the concert he became the pupil and friend of Hector Berlioz, who encouraged him both as virtuoso and composer. The next year (1846–1847) Gottschalk appeared with Berlioz in a series of concerts at the Théâtre des Italiens. Berlioz described his playing like this:

> Gottschalk is one of the very small number who possess all the different elements of a consummate pianist—all the facilities which surround him with

an irresistible prestige, and give a sovereign power.
. . . There is an exquisite grace in manner of phrasing sweet melodies and throwing light touches from the higher keys. The boldness, the brilliancy and the originality of his playing at once dazzles and astonishes. . . .

For the next six years Gottschalk toured the continent achieving a success that rivaled that of any other piano virtuoso of the time. His popularity approached that of Franz Liszt, and the young American was welcomed at all the Old World musical centers.

At all of his concerts Gottschalk included his own compositions, many of which were based upon musical recollections of songs and dances he had heard as a boy. In this music Gottschalk attempted to create a New World complement to European nationalism, utilizing the dances he had heard in New Orleans in the same way Chopin used the Polish mazurka and Liszt used the Hungarian czardas.

After conquering the musical world of Europe, Gottschalk returned home in 1853. He was twenty-four years old at the time and had been abroad for twelve years. On February 11, 1853, he made his debut as a mature artist in the ballroom of Niblo's Garden in New York City. The success of the concert was attested to by none other than P. T. Barnum, the circus impresario, who offered the pianist a contract guaranteeing him a minimum of $20,000, plus expenses, and a percentage of the receipts, for a six-month tour.

Gottschalk turned down the offer, but did embark on a spectacularly successful concert career in America under the management of Max Strakosch. He gave a prodigious number of concerts on his American tours. In the year 1862–1863, for example, he appeared no less than eleven hundred times in concerts both in America and Canada. He played everywhere, performing to vast audiences in cities, towns, and backwoods settlements, often playing as many as three or four concerts in the same day.

He amassed a fortune through his concertizing, but his personal extravagance and generosity dissipated most of his wealth. He spent money lavishly on food, clothing, jewelry, and travel, often reserving an entire floor in the finest hotel for his entourage. Gottschalk was also generous to a fault. He gave money to practically anyone who asked him for help and played at numerous benefit concerts for all kinds of worthy causes.

While on tour in South America in 1869 Gottschalk contracted yellow fever. Although he fought the ravages of the disease for some months, he finally succumbed. He died in the town of Tijuca, a suburb of Rio de Janeiro, where he was taken after a relapse on

Much of Gottschalk's work reflects the creole music of his native New Orleans. Below, a performance of the bamboula.

the morning of December 18, 1869. All of Brazil went into mourning for the dead musician and the newspapers printed glowing eulogies. His remains were taken to New York and placed in Greenwood Cemetery.

In many respects Gottschalk remains an enigmatic figure in American music. As a virtuoso pianist he won the acclaim of the entire world. He was also the first musician of international stature whom the New World produced. His music was appreciated and widely played, and in his compositions Gottschalk was completely American. He recognized the vitality and exuberance of American folk music and utilized this invention in his music. Why then, was he not an American Glinka? Why was he not the initiator of an impulse toward exploring and exploiting the American experience?

Certainly, all the elements for this kind of a development were there; Gottschalk was a world-renowned virtuoso and composer who successfully incorporated native American themes in his work. But no one followed in his wake. It remained for the Bohemian Dvořák to awaken America's composers to the richness that had been around them all this time. Gottschalk today remains an exotic, lonely figure, isolated from the mainstreams of American musical development. He was the first to appreciate the musical significance of the cakewalk, the bamboula, and the creole songs of his native New Orleans. But his appreciation was premature, for the rest of America was not ready to follow his lead.

10. A FLOWERING IN NEW ORLEANS

WHILE the learned professors in New York and Boston were in the midst of their agonizing reappraisal of the role of art music in American cultural life, a new kind of music that had taken shape during the years following the Civil War was being heard in the saloons and honky-tonks of New Orleans. The untutored musicians who played this music were blithely unaware of the upheaval shaking the foundations of American art music. Yet both events were destined to dominate American music in the twentieth century.

Today, when musicologists discuss the American contribution to the world's musical heritage, most will agree upon the significance of jazz as an indigenous musical form. In many respects jazz is akin to folk music. It grew on its own in response to the musical needs of a particular segment of the American population. Jazz was, in its initial stages, the secular music

of the American Negro. Initially, commercial considerations had little if any influence on this development.

Like so much of American music, jazz represents a
synthesis, a coming-together of various musical traditions and styles. In this sense jazz is a musical hybrid,
exhibiting an almost biological hybrid vitality. It
drew upon all the melodic and rhythmic resources of
the New World.

In jazz we can recognize traces of Baptist hymns and
Elizabethan ballads; we hear echoes of Negro spirituals, of blues and the old field holler. Jazz rhythms
contain hints of the French quadrille along with the
syncopated rhythm of ragtime; we can distinguish
traces of the foot-tapping pulse of the country hoe-
down and mountain reel of Scotch-Irish derivation
along with the memory of a complex and sophisticated
African percussive tradition. All of these elements
were assimilated and transformed in the formation of
that musical flowering called jazz.

Nor was this a sudden, overnight development. It
took some two centuries for the synthesis to be completed. Its history can be traced through the successive
waves of music that spread from the Negro community—from African tribal music to plantation slave
songs, the minstrel show, and ragtime.

According to tradition jazz came into being in the
bawdy-houses of New Orleans' Storyville. More ac-
curately, jazz was "in the air" at the turn of the century. Something very much like jazz was being
performed at that time wherever Negro musicians

In jazz we hear echoes of Negro spirituals, of blues, and the old field holler.

found opportunity to play, for, as "Jelly Roll" Morton, one of the pioneers of jazz, described the situation: "Jazz music is a style, not a composition." It was a style that reflected a people and not a particular city or locale.

The focal point for this development, however, became New Orleans. There was good reason for this. New Orleans, at the time, was a tolerant, fun-loving city in whose exuberant life even a lowly black musician might find a place. The annual Mardi Gras, the colorful processions and numerous parades and celebrations that characterized the city, placed a premium upon musicians of all kinds.

After the Civil War and emancipation many Negroes turned to music as a means of earning their livelihoods. Many Negroes already were musicians for, as we have seen, the Negro musician was a regular feature of plantation life. More important, music provided one of the few areas in which a black man was permitted to excel.

Immediately following the Civil War, bands of newly emancipated street musicians appeared throughout the South. They sang, danced, and performed, usually to the accompaniment of banjo, guitar, and bones—the traditional instruments of the Negro musician in the South. Many of these street musicians made their way to New Orleans where they hoped they might be accepted more readily than elsewhere in the South.

Here their musical horizons were broadened significantly. For one thing New Orleans had been a center for the manufacture of wind instruments for many years. These were plentiful and inexpensive, especially since a large store of surplus band instruments from both the Confederate and Union armies had come onto the market. The price of a serviceable instrument came within the range of practically anyone who wanted to make music.

The availability of these instruments, together with a large audience for music, led to the organization of bands. No other city in America had so marked a sympathy for band music. In the decades following the Civil War, the sound of the brass band became the hallmark of New Orleans. Bands were everywhere. They accompanied funerals, religious and secular processions, patriotic parades, weddings, excursions, and carnivals. Bands from New Orleans entertained on the big Mississippi River boats. Bands were used to advertise sales and political speeches. Many of these bands were made up of Negro musicians. A dozen Negro bands took part in the mammoth funeral cortege for President Garfield in 1881.

We do not know for sure how these Negro bands played. That is, we cannot be certain to what extent they conformed to conventional standards. We do know, from descriptive accounts of the period, that they did not sound like the usual military band. We also know that the Negro bands were very popular with all the people of New Orleans. White musicians of the time complained bitterly about this preference.

These Negro street bands were made up, for the most part, of musicians who worked at other trades and played in their spare time. Most of them learned their instruments without benefit of formal training. They learned through trial and error, through a continual process of experimentation. In this way new techniques of performance evolved, full of unorthodox sounds and timbres that were never taught in conventional study.

Gradually a distinct style of performance evolved. Very few of these musicians could read music and they were compelled to play by "ear" rather than "eye." Guided only by their musical intuition and the inspiration of the moment, they transformed popular songs and tunes through the unrestricted play of their intelligence and imagination. Thus they brought to their music new tonal combinations, never-before-heard dissonances, novel melodic figures, and disjointed counterpoints.

They also brought the peculiar qualities and devices

129

of Negro singing techniques to this music. In their playing they emulated the harsh, guttural, throaty sounds they used in singing. In so doing, they created a new kind of instrumental tone.

When these instrumental techniques were applied to the syncopated rhythms of ragtime, jazz came into being. Blatant, abandoned, full of driving energy and imaginative, often outrageous, invention, this was a music calculated to shock the sensibilities of genteel America. In New Orleans, however, it flourished. This was the music that resounded in such notorious pleasure domes as *The 101 Ranch, Pete La La's Cafe,* and *The Tuxedo Dance Hall.*

Haunts such as these, along Basin Street in the notorious Storyville section of New Orleans, provided the Negro musician opportunities for employment which no other city or district could match. It is not surprising that black musicians flocked to this city. Although they were not particularly well paid for their services, and even the best had to double at other jobs, they were encouraged and even, at times, idolized. In Storyville the black musician was afforded the stimulation and acceptance necessary to develop his highly personal style and technique. In Storyville the jazz musician was king.

One of the earliest names associated with classic New Orleans jazz is that of Charles "Buddy" Bolden. Tall, slender, strikingly handsome, Bolden was a barber with his own shop and the publisher of a scandal sheet called *The Cricket.* He learned to play the cornet by himself and organized a band early in the

1890's. Although he never learned how to read music, Bolden soon demonstrated his musical abilities. His inventiveness and approach won immediate popularity and the Bolden band came into wide demand for parades and dances.

For almost fifteen years the Bolden band provided a focal point for New Orleans music. At one time or another most of the important jazz pioneers played with Bolden. His reputation became so important that for years afterward jazz musicians boasted of their association with him.

According to Louis Armstrong, Bolden was a "one man genius—way ahead of them all." It was said that on a quiet day you could hear the sound of his cornet for miles. His ability to improvise and embroider a melody with all kinds of exuberant turns and ornaments was an unforgettable aural experience.

Bolden continued to be a dominant figure in New Orleans jazz right up to the time of his tragic breakdown. While playing in a street parade in 1907, Bolden suffered a nervous collapse. He had to be confined to a sanitarium, where he remained till his death in 1931. Although his career was cut short at the height of his powers, Bolden left a significant legacy. He, more than any other figure, gave form to the shapeless mélange of musical styles and syntax that grew out of the experience of the Negro ghetto.

After the loss of Bolden, Freddie Keppard (1883–1932) became the dominant figure in New Orleans jazz. An outstanding cornet player, in 1909 he organized the Olympia Band, which reigned as the leading

Sidney Bechet, one of the outstanding performers of New Orleans jazz.

musical organization until the close of Storyville in 1917. Included in this small band—the classic jazz ensemble was rarely larger than seven pieces—were such outstanding musicians as Louis "Big Eye" Nelson (clarinet), Sidney Bechet (clarinet), Willy Santiago (guitar), Zue Robertson (trombone), and King Oliver (cornet).

There were, of course, many other bands in New Orleans at this time and they share in the credit for the development of jazz. It was a bustling time when the city seemed to be bursting with creative energy. Competition between bands as well as individual musicians was intense. Bands played all over the city for practically every public affair. Occasionally, two or more bands, each with its own following of admirers, would cross in the street. Such an event generally led to a "cutting match"—a musical free-for-all—in which individual bands would try to outdo each other in sheer volume of sound as well as improvisational invention.

These early jazz musicians used whatever songs and melodies were currently popular as springboards for their invention. All music was grist for the jazz mill— patriotic songs, bawdy-house ballads, music hall tunes, religious hymns, blues, French and Spanish dances, minstrel songs. Everything and anything was utilized in this musical stew. This caldronlike quality of early jazz was described by "Jelly Roll" Morton in an account of his own version of "Tiger Rag":

> The Tiger Rag I transformed from an old French quadrille, which was originally in a lot of different tempos. First, there was the introduction—"everybody get your partners"—and the people would go rushing around the hall. . . . The next strain would be a waltz . . . then another strain which comes right behind the waltz in mazooka time. . . . We had two other strains in two-four time. I transformed these into the *Tiger Rag* which I also named from the way I made the "Tiger" roar with my elbow! . . . In one of my earliest tunes, *New Orleans Blues,* you can notice the Spanish tinge. . . . In fact, if you can't put tinges of Spanish into your tunes, you will never be able to get the right seasoning, I call it, for jazz. . . .

It was in this kind of creative atmosphere that the

pattern of jazz was established. The music was a mélange of current styles and songs, but the typical or-
chestration derives from the blues. There is an early
recording, dating back to 1911 or 1912, of a typical
blues song of the period called "When a 'Gaitor Hollers," sung by Margaret Johnson accompanied by
clarinet, cornet, and piano. The instrumentalists are
not named, though the cornet player is believed to be
King Oliver.

In this record Margaret Johnson carries the melodic
lead, while the two instruments play discreetly under
her voice. The piano is used as a rhythm instrument
providing a steady beat that underlies the performance. In the "breaks" between voice verses, the cornet
comes up with its own strident solos, answering the
voice with sighs, sobs, and an occasional chuckle. The
strident whine of the clarinet reinforces this effect
when the two instruments join in these bridges, in
discordant duets.

Singer, clarinet, and cornet provide a three-part harmony in a call-and-response pattern that is still fundamental to the music of West Africa. Take the singer
away, add a trombone, and you still have three voices
that sing and answer the melody over a throbbing
rhythm.

Cornet, trumpet, clarinet, and trombone were the
instruments favored by the early jazzmen as the most
flexible and expressive. The trumpet or cornet generally took the lead "voice," sounding the calls to
which the other instruments responded. Clarinet (high
voice) and trombone (low voice) completed the three-
part harmony. Their voices embroider around the

lead melody and take their own melodic breaks in turn.

Rhythm came to consist generally of guitar, bass, and drums, while some of the early bands included banjo and an occasional tuba to round out the rhythm section. Later the piano was incorporated as a dual instrument—the left hand providing a percussive beat while the right hand allowed for another melodic voice.

The New Orleans period of jazz ended in 1913 when all the saloons and dance halls in Storyville were closed because of a brawl in which two men were killed. Deprived of their livelihood, jazz musicians began to flow from New Orleans in a mass exodus. By the time Storyville was back in business again in late 1914, most of the musicians had already left and there were few to mourn its official demise in 1917. New Orleans musicians streamed north to play in the cabarets and night clubs of St. Louis and Chicago, Memphis and New York. Most of them were welcomed. America had had a taste of jazz through the efforts of touring bands, especially those organized by King Oliver and Freddie Keppard, and demanded more of this heady music.

In 1918 King Oliver settled in Chicago, where he organized his influential Creole Jazz Band, which included Jimmy Noone (clarinet), Honore Dutry (trombone), Ed Garland (bass), Lillian Hardin (piano), and Minor "Ram" Hall (drums). In 1922 Oliver added a second cornet to the band, a young player from New Orleans named Louis Armstrong.

Above, Fletcher Henderson (at the piano) in 1924; Coleman Hawkins is leaning on the chair. Lower left, Louis Armstrong. Lower right, Duke Ellington.

In the early twenties the Creole Jazz Band made a series of recordings which provide the definitive sound of classic New Orleans jazz. Such songs as "Dipper-mouth Blues," "High Society," "Canal Street Blues," and "Snake Rag" reveal the rhythmic and melodic flexibility that was at the heart of the style. The playing is spontaneous, relaxed, and perfectly controlled, demonstrating the freedom and inventiveness of this home-grown musical form.

The Chicago period saw a further development of jazz style. In its earliest phase the rhythmic base was provided by the military drum and revolved around a whole-note beat. During the first decade of the twentieth century a half-note beat with syncopation gradually came to be the preferred meter. Between 1910 and 1930 this half-note meter was broken up, occasionally with a tango-like syncopation, until by the late 1920's Louis Armstrong had made a quarter-note rhythm irrevocable.

The next important phase in the history of jazz takes us to New York City. In 1919 a Negro pianist from Georgia named Fletcher Henderson organized a radically different kind of jazz band which played at the Roseland dance hall. Henderson's band was big, featuring as many as twenty-five individual musicians. The sheer size of the band made individual improvisation, which had been at the heart of jazz till this time, impossible. Groups of more than nine players cannot achieve the spontaneous cohesion and the smooth ensemble necessary for an improvisational jazz performance.

Instead Henderson prepared orchestral arrangements, written out in advance and carefully rehearsed before the performance. What Henderson's band lost in spontaneity was made up in sonority and the rich musical effects that could be generated by a large number of instruments playing simultaneously.

More important, Henderson's big band was commercially successful. The public responded to the rich sound and driving rhythm generated by this kind of ensemble. Roseland became a center for this new kind of jazz and the crowds that were drawn to this New York dance hall inspired an avalanche of imitators. The Henderson band played in Roseland for almost fifteen years and included in its roster some of the finest jazz musicians of the time, including Louis Armstrong and Coleman Hawkins.

Another important influence on this kind of big-band, formalized jazz was Edward "Duke" Ellington. Born in Washington, D.C., in 1899, Ellington studied music at the Pratt Institute in that city and formed his first band, a small one, in 1918. Although this band followed the popular New Orleans style of the period, Ellington had definite ideas about the direction jazz was going to take, and these did not include individual improvisation. From the beginning he tried to create a personal style, an individual expression in the tradition of art composers.

A talented composer and arranger, Ellington quickly rose to national and international fame. He toured Europe with immense success in 1933. His compositions are marked by sophistication, rhythmic smoothness, and originality and include what many musicologists consider masterpieces of jazz-inspired orchestral compositions. Constant Lambert, the English composer-musicologist, described Ellington as "the first jazz composer of distinction."

The work of Henderson and Ellington pointed the way. By the end of the 1920's and the beginning of the 1930's the big band dominated jazz. What happened was that large dance bands were commercially successful while the small hot groups were not. This situation came to a peak in the over-blown, slick ensembles exploited by Paul Whiteman and other musical impresarios in the mid-1930's. This new sound was called swing, and it swept the nation.

Jazz, in the New Orleans tradition of spontaneous improvisation, practically disappeared in the face of this slick competition. Eddie Condon, the noted jazz guitarist, summed up the situation: "Just about the only place we could play was in our own rooms, at our own request."

A generation of musicians grew up in the 1930's, chafing at the bit imposed by the big-band concept of swing. Brilliant and beautiful and slick as the big band was, it was also completely removed from the original feeling of jazz. The inspired performer was lost in the sections of the big band and had to settle for informal "jam" sessions, held in the privacy of the dressing room between shows, to create any kind of personal expression.

An instrumental revolt against the big band began to take shape and was in full swing by the mid-1940's.

Some important innovators of "modern" jazz. Above left, Charlie Parker; above right, Dizzy Gillespie; below, Thelonius Monk. Facing page: above left, Sonny Rollins; above right, Miles Davis; below, Ornette Coleman. Coleman's interpretations are considered to be the last word in "cool" jazz.

The result was a return to the improvisational tradition of early New Orleans jazz—with one big difference. The musicians who instituted the revolt were more capable, in every aspect of musicianship and instrumental competence, than their untutored predecessors. All were musically literate, with a theoretical background in music and a solid instrumental foundation: these were the professional requirements.

They brought this musical sophistication to improvisational jazz with startling results. Spearheaded by musicians of the caliber of Charlie Parker, Thelonius Monk, Dizzy Gillespie, their music exploded into an astonishingly brilliant glissando of abstract sound.

This development marked an important turning point in the development of jazz, an advance that took jazz from its traditional role of a popular-folk music form into the more ethereal realm of art. Until this time jazz was primarily dance music. It was performed to be danced to and its basic function was to involve the listener in active physical participation. As such its musical development was severely restricted by the demands of the dance floor.

During the 1940's jazz—improvisational jazz performed by small, intimate groups—was liberated from the dance floor. It became music for listening. The inventive brilliance of Charlie Parker was a prime moving force in this direction. Parker had original ideas about rhythm, melody, and phrase length, and a sweeping melodic and harmonic imagination.

As a result of Parker's vision the rhythm section provided a new function in the expression of the jazz ensemble. It gave up the steady metronomic pulse and took the drummer's foot off the bass pedal, allowing the rhythm section the freedom necessary to accent the new rhythms that the soloists were generating in their improvisational flights. The new sound was called "bop"—after a rhythmic device—and it found an enthusiastic audience all over the world.

This new jazz language was formalized and further refined in the 1950's. Jazz became "cool" as epitomized in a group of orchestral recordings made by trumpeter Miles Davis with a medium-sized group. This phase was marked by rhythmic freedom and a sophisticated harmonic development. One of the members of Davis's group was John Lewis, who later organized the Modern Jazz Quartet, a jazz-improvisation group that adapted and assimilated aspects of classic counterpoint and harmonic development.

Another pioneer during this period was Thelonius Monk whose compositions for small groups, such as "Four In One" and "Criss Cross," introduced the idea of thematically developed improvisation, rather than harmonic, as a form within the jazz tradition. Exploiting this basic idea, tenor saxophonist Theodore "Sonny" Rollins became one of the first horn players in jazz to perform an extended improvisation with thematic development and cohesion.

This line was developed further by Charlie Mingus, the bassist, who combined composition and improvisation in a manner suggesting early jazz styles. Ornette Coleman has probably carried the "cool" style of jazz to its greatest extreme to date. Coleman's most important innovations are rhythmic and have introduced a concept of almost African subtlety to group playing.

In Coleman's groups drummer and bass may play entirely different rhythmic patterns, simultaneously, against a rhythm generated by the solo instruments out of the phrasing of their improvised melodic lines.

Intonation in the Coleman style is also free, with the traditional "blue" notes and vocalized inflections elevated to a point where they encompass whole melodic phrases and lines. Improvisation in the Coleman style is based on a general thematic outline rather than on the harmonic progression of a theme melody. This style represents a triumph of improvisation over all other aspects of musical structure.

This, then, is a brief history of jazz and it is one of the most exciting chapters in all of music. What began as "the bottom-waving, vulgar, barbaric howl" has been transformed into a sophisticated, even esoteric expression. Jazz has moved from the saloon to the concert hall, and in the process it has brought improvisation back to the concert hall where it had all but disappeared since the baroque period.

This has taken place within a time span of no more than fifty years. During all of this time, jazz has exerted a continuous influence upon all aspects of American music. Its beat, its swing, its earthiness, have provided the base upon which the entire structure of modern popular music has been erected. Its harmonic and rhythmic inventiveness have found their way into the art compositions of composers all over the world. Although jazz today hardly qualifies as "popular" music—it is too highly evolved and sophisticated—it has left its mark and its sound indelibly etched into the music of the twentieth century.

11. GERSHWIN AND IVES: THE TRIUMPH OF THE POPULAR SPIRIT

TWO IMPORTANT developments followed in the wake of Dvořák's liberating evocation of the popular spirit. One was the growth of a distinctive art music which resulted from this belated recognition of the artistic validity of the American experience. The other was the dramatic development of jazz. At first sight, these would appear to have little to do with one another. Certainly this New Orleans saloon music would seem to have little in common with events taking place in the academy. Yet both represent high points in the growth of a distinctive American music.

In the academy this important advance was represented by the recognition of an American folk tradition. Jazz marks a culmination of the popular spirit. It generated an indigenous sound, expressive of the unique energy of the New World. These two elements were to combine in the music of one of America's most influential, versatile, composers, George Gershwin.

Not surprisingly, in view of the split development of American music, George Gershwin did not begin his career as an art composer. Throughout most of his life Gershwin was a writer of popular songs and musical comedy. As such he functioned and was shaped in the mainstream of professional American entertainment. His talent, however, was such that it could not be confined to the music hall and spilled over, almost without volition, into the world of art.

In this sense Gershwin is closer to the composers of the baroque and early classical period. Like Scarlatti, Haydn, or Mozart, he did not compose primarily to express his innermost soul. He wrote, instead, for the purpose of pleasing an audience. He was a professional, rather than an artist, who wrote music designed to appeal to the broadest possible audience.

Actually, in the history of music, this attitude is the more venerable one. The idea of "art"—in the sense of music composed for its own sake alone—is a comparatively modern concept. It began, really, with Beethoven, and was further defined in the romantic period. This school reached a peak in the overblown pretensions of the late nineteenth-century Germanic tradition.

Like so many important musical figures George Gershwin revealed his talents early and was reported to have been able to pick out tunes on the family piano before he was three years old. He was born in Brooklyn, New York, on September 26, 1898, to a poor Russian-Jewish immigrant family. As a boy his obvious talents were encouraged and he studied the piano with Charles Hambitzer and Ernest Hutcheson. Later, he studied harmony and composition with Edward Elenyi, and Rubin Goldmark who had been a pupil of Dvořák's.

By the time he was fourteen Gershwin was already playing professionally as a demonstration pianist with a music-publishing firm. He had also begun to write his first songs. These early attempts were climaxed by his composition of a complete musical comedy which he finished before he was nineteen. *La La Lucille* was produced on Broadway in 1919.

Although neither a commercial nor a critical success, *La La Lucille* revealed the promise of a strikingly original talent. It also brought the young composer to the attention of George White, the theatrical producer, who commissioned Gershwin to write the music for the *George White Scandals,* which opened in 1922. He wrote the song "Swanee" for this revue. Given a sparkling reading in the production by the singer Al Jolson, the song became the biggest hit of the year. At the age of twenty-four Gershwin was propelled into national prominence—a position from which he never retreated for the rest of his life.

During the next decade the name George Gershwin became a permanent fixture on Broadway marquees. After the success of his music for the *George White Scandals,* Gershwin went on to compose the scores for a brilliant string of musical comedies that included *Lady Be Good* (1924), *Tip Toes* (1925), *Oh, Kay* (1926), *Funny Face* (1927), and *Girl Crazy* (1930).

George Gershwin, a brilliant composer and pianist, often conducted performances of his music.

Then, in collaboration with his brother Ira, who wrote the lyrics for his songs, Gershwin turned his talents to satire. *Strike Up The Band* (1930) marked a sharp departure from the style and content of his earlier works. It was topical, satiric, and pointedly concerned with contemporary social problems. This was followed by another musical in the same vein, *Of Thee I Sing* (1931), which spoofed the folklore of an American presidential election and its White House aftermath. This production was awarded the first Pulitzer Prize ever given for a musical comedy.

Of Thee I Sing was followed in 1933 by another savage musical satire, *Let 'em Eat Cake,* with a libretto by Kaufman and Ryskind and lyrics by Ira Gershwin. This production was described by Brooks Atkinson, critic of the *New York Times,* as hardly deserving the title *comedy* since the authors' "hatreds have triumphed over their sense of humor."

As a composer of popular songs and musical comedy George Gershwin was fabulously successful. His scores in this genre dominated Broadway for more than a decade and were a primary influence on the development of American musical comedy. Working for the most part within the severe limitations of commercially oriented Tin Pan Alley, Gershwin had the rare ability to breathe fresh life into old musical clichés. He, more than any other popular composer, could write music that resembled the prevalent stereotypes enough to be acceptable to a popular audience, while at the same time giving the formula the slight twist of originality that can transform it into an unexpectedly fresh and adult experience. At their best Gershwin's songs are ironic, energetic, and project a sense of pathos that strikes a responsive chord in the listener. They remain today among the finest popular songs written by an American.

An important turning point in Gershwin's career came in 1924 when Paul Whiteman commissioned him to write a piece of music of symphonic proportions that would embody jazz elements. Gershwin became fired with the idea and completed the piano score of his *Rhapsody in Blue* within three weeks. At the première of the rhapsody on February 12, 1924, Whiteman conducted and Gershwin was the piano soloist.

In form and style Gershwin borrowed liberally from Franz Liszt for the composition of his rhapsody. He used jazz in exactly the same way that Liszt used Hungarian gypsy music in his rhapsodies. There is also something of Tschaikowsky in Gershwin's score, especially in the treatment of the slow section. Despite this obvious eclecticism Gershwin's rhapsody was strikingly original in concept and execution. In this work Gershwin combined elements of popular style and conventional art forms in a fusion of remarkable felicity and vitality.

Actually, several European composers, notably Stravinsky and Milhaud, had anticipated the possibilities inherent in jazz, and both had used some of its musical effects in their compositions with considerable success. But there was an important difference in their utilization of this American form. For a European, jazz was an exotic expression that was foreign to his experience. For Gershwin, whose musical talents were formed in the caldron of American popular music, jazz was more natural. Jazz was a basic element of the tradition in which Gershwin functioned. This attitude is reflected in his own thoughts about jazz: "Jazz is music," Gershwin wrote.

"It uses the same notes that Bach used. When jazz is played in another country it is called American. When it is played by foreign musicians, it sounds false. Jazz is the result of the energy stored up in America. . . . Jazz has contributed an enduring value to America in the sense that it has expressed ourselves. It is an original American achievement that will endure. . . . I believe that it can be made the basis of serious symphonic works of lasting value, in the hands of a composer with a talent for both jazz and symphonic music. . . ." So successful was *Rhapsody In Blue,* in terms of both critical and public acceptance, that Gershwin was commissioned to write another symphonic work by Walter Damrosch, then conductor of the Philharmonic-Symphony Orchestra of New York. For this occasion Gershwin wrote his Concerto in F for piano and orchestra. It was first performed on December 3, 1925, in New York City, with Gershwin as soloist.

During this time Gershwin played a dual musical role. He was both a commercially successful writer of musical comedy and popular songs and a "serious" composer. Through his work Tin Pan Alley gained a niche in Carnegie Hall, and a substantial one at that. In 1930 the English conductor-musicologist, Albert Coates, included the piano concerto in his compilation of the best musical compositions of all time. This was the only work by an American composer to appear on the list. Today, more than forty years after its première, Gershwin's concerto is firmly entrenched as the first work of this kind by an American composer to have entered the permanent repertoire of symphonic music.

Gershwin's next "serious" work was an orchestral tone poem titled *An American In Paris*. An energetic, brash composition, colorfully and realistically orchestrated—Gershwin used real Paris taxi horns in the score—the work was an immediate success. It was first performed by the Philharmonic-Symphony Orchestra of New York in Carnegie Hall, on December 13, 1928. Since that time it has been played regularly by symphonic orchestras all over the world.

In 1931, while Gershwin was in Hollywood, he wrote the music for the film comedy *Delicious*. One sequence in the film featured a New York City street scene. Gershwin wrote what he called a "rivet theme" for this sequence to express the dynamic energy and bustle of the city. Later he used this theme as the basis for his next symphonic work which he first called *Rhapsody In Rivets*. Renamed *Second Rhapsody*, the composition was first performed by the Boston Symphony Orchestra under the direction of Serge Koussevitzky on January 29, 1932. Mechanistic percussive treatment, syncopated dance rhythms, and Tin Pan Alley tune clichés were all exploited in this musical interpretation of the "Big City."

The *Cuban Overture,* written in 1934, was Gershwin's last and least successful orchestral work. In all of his symphonic compositions Gershwin's sense of melody and feel for vernacular music triumphs over what, in the final analysis, was an inadequate compositional technique. The tunes and the treatment are so good that neither Gershwin's clumsy attempts at "development" nor the romantic tinsel with which they are flimsily tied together could detract from the overall power of these works. As a matter of fact, this power has kept them very much alive and they are still performed in concert halls throughout the world.

Gershwin's most successful work, however, achieves a convincing fulfillment as art. This, of course, is *Porgy and Bess,* the "super musical" which soared beyond the limits of musical comedy to take its place as what many musicologists consider the finest American opera ever written.

In this work the two conflicting aspects of Gershwin's musical career are resolved. Here the man of commerce (the successful tunesmith who had made literally millions out of his music) and the man of art (who wished to leave a legacy to a future America) became one. Here the superb tunesmith became the consummate artist.

Porgy and Bess is, first of all, a work for the theatre, a medium which could allow scope for all of Gershwin's considerable experience and training. As a composer Gershwin was always most comfortable in terms of the theatre. His purely orchestral music, on the other hand, was always somewhat forced in its organization and form. Gershwin created theatrical music spontaneously, naturally, whereas his orchestral creation always has the blemish of effort.

The story was based on the novel *Porgy* by DuBose

Heyward, which dealt with Negro life in Charleston, South Carolina. Heyward, himself, prepared the libretto for the opera with the composer's brother collaborating on the lyrics for the songs. As far as Gershwin was concerned, *Porgy and Bess* was a full-fledged opera and he took the composition very seriously.

To prepare himself for the job Gershwin spent the summer of 1934 on Folly Island, about ten miles from Charleston, where he could listen to and absorb the music and folkways of the Negroes living on the island. He attended religious services and took part in "shouts"; he listened to the songs of fishermen and farm hands; he was fascinated by the peculiar cries of Negro street vendors and captured their melodic inflections on the stage.

Porgy and Bess was first performed at the Colonial Theatre in Boston, on September 30, 1935, in a production of the Theatre Guild. Stage direction was by Rouben Mamoulian, and Alexander Smallens conducted. On October 10, it was brought to the Alvin Theater in New York where it ran for sixteen weeks. It has been revived regularly since that beginning, and a company with an all-Negro cast took it on a European tour in 1952 and played to thunderous acclaim in all the capitals of Europe.

At first *Porgy* was considered nothing more than a "super musical" by many American critics. But in Europe the stature of the work was quickly recognized and it has been incorporated into the repertoire of most of the leading "grand" opera companies where it is regularly staged.

George Gershwin died in Hollywood on July 1, 1937, after an unsuccessful brain operation. During his tragically short career Gershwin produced a remarkably prolific body of work. He wrote some of our most popular songs, symphonic works that have been accepted into the standard repertoire, a series of brilliant musical comedies, and *Porgy and Bess,* his masterpiece.

In all of his work Gershwin's concern with American musical roots is evident. His symphonic compositions and opera mark the triumph of the popular spirit in the art music of America. He elevated the peculiar American genius for popular expression to the highest musical plane. Herein lies Gershwin's principal contribution to American music and the factor that will assure his continued popularity and acclaim.

Whereas George Gershwin worked in the glare of critical and commercial success, Charles Ives worked in obscurity. Though Ives created the bulk of his output before Gershwin appeared on the scene, his music was almost completely neglected until he was "rediscovered" in the 1940's and 1950's. He earned his livelihood, for most of his adult life, in the insurance business and created some of the most striking examples of American music in his spare time. Ives's composing was restricted to weekends, holidays, vacations, and long evenings.

Ives, himself, was quite philosophic about this and never considered his business career a handicap to artistic production. On the contrary, he regarded his music and the business in which he earned his livelihood as complementary activities: "My work in business helped my music and my work in music helped my business."

He also went on to say:

> . . . a man could keep his music interest keener, stronger, bigger and freer if he didn't try to make a living out of it. Assuming that a man lives by himself and with no dependents, no one to feed but himself, and is willing to live as simply as Thoreau, he might write music that no one would play prettily [pretty and nice were two of Ives's most damning adjectives], listen to, or buy. But—if he has a wife and some children, how can he let his children starve on his dissonances? So he has to weaken—and if he is a man, *should* weaken for his children—but his music . . . more than weakens— it goes ta-ta for money! Bad for him, bad for music!

Charles Ives was born in Danbury, Connecticut, on October 20, 1874. His father was a bandmaster by profession and young Ives grew up in an atmosphere where music was as ubiquitous as air. He received his earliest musical training from his father and began playing instruments by the time he was five. In time Ives mastered several instruments including piano, violin, and organ. He began playing professionally when he was twelve, as organist in a local church.

Although the family was professionally involved in Danbury's musical life there was little of the "refinement" or "culture," which was so typical of that period, in the Ives household. In musical terms this household centered around the town band, ragtime, corny theatre tunes, chapel hymns, camp meeting songs, country dances—in the living music that reflected the life of a small Connecticut town in the tail end of the nineteenth century.

Despite this popular outlook Ives's musical education was in no way limited. Ives's father also instilled a respect for the "manly" composers: Handel, Beethoven, Bach, and Brahms. He gave young Charles his first training in harmony, counterpoint, and the fugue. The senior Ives had an inquiring mind and an open ear and encouraged these qualities in his son. When Charles was ten his father had him sing "Swanee River" in the key of E flat major while playing the accompaniment in the key of C major, in order to "stretch our ears."

The elder Ives also had a novel approach to music as he did to all aural experience. He constructed a device out of a sound box and violin strings with which to play quarter-tone intervals, just to hear what they sounded like. He listened for those peculiarities of sound and style in the singing and playing of his fellow townsmen that expressed their spirit and individuality. Charles Ives later quoted his father in describing an incident that typified his novel approach to music. When he was once asked how he could stand listening to Old John (the local stonemason) bellowing off-key at camp meetings, he answered: "Old John is a supreme musician. Look into his face while he sings and hear the music of the ages. Don't pay too much attention to the sounds. If you do, you may miss the music."

This attitude became central to the music of Charles

Ives. He always listened for the "music" rather than the sounds and in so doing discovered a world of inspiration in his own back yard. This at a time when academic American composers were looking everywhere for inspiration but home.

What excited Ives's imagination most of all was the vast body of living music rooted in the Yankee tradition of Danbury. He listened to the congregation singing to his organ on Sundays, each untutored voice croaking a slightly different version of the same hymn tune at the same time. He tried to capture this spirit in his compositions:

> If a Yankee can reflect the fervency with which the gospels were sung—the fervency of Aunt Sarah, who scrubbed her life away for her brother's ten orphans, the fervency with which this woman, after a fourteen-hour work day on the farm, would hitch up and drive five miles through the mud and rain to a prayer-meeting—her one articulate outlet for the fullness of her unselfish soul—if he can reflect the fervency of such a spirit, he may find there a local color which will do all the world good. If his music can but catch that spirit by being a part with itself, it will come somewhere near this idea—and it will be American too. . . .

Barn dances and country hoedowns, amateur town bands and local musical performances particularly fascinated Ives. He listened for the chance occurrence, the spontaneous mistake or accident which produced weird, undreamed-of effects of harmonic and rhythmic dislocation. He described such an occurrence:

I remember hearing, when a boy, the music of a band in which players were arranged in two or three groups around the town square. The main group in the bandstand at the center usually played the main themes, while the others, from neighboring roofs and verandahs, played the variations, refrains and so forth. . . . The bandmaster told of a man who, living nearer the variations, insisted that they were the real music and that it was more beautiful to hear the tune come sifting through them than the other way around. Others, walking around the square were surprised at the different and interesting effects they got as they changed positions. . . .

Charles Ives began composing almost as soon as he began playing instruments. When he was fourteen the town band performed a piece of his which "suggested a Steve Foster tune, while over it the old farmers fiddled a barn dance with all its jigs, gallops, and reels." Later Ives used this theme in his Second Symphony which he began working on in 1897.

At twenty, the year he entered Yale, he wrote a *Song for the Harvest Season,* for voice, cornet, trombone, and organ pedal—each in a different key! This song was written in 1894, a time when even the most advanced European composers had not yet begun to experiment with polytonality. Stravinsky used the polytonic technique in *Petrouchka,* creating a furor at its Paris première, almost twenty years later, in 1911.

These were the background and unconventional interests Ives brought to Yale in 1894. Here he studied harmony and composition with Horatio Parker and

One of America's most original composers, Charles Ives explored atonality and the simultaneous playing of multiple melodies. His work includes four major symphonies.

soon learned that his musical vision was far different from that of the academy. When he submitted his first composition to Professor Parker, the teacher took one look at the complex score and suggested that Ives refrain from "hogging all the keys at one meal." After that the daring young man from Danbury realized he had to keep his musical ideas to himself. He satisfied academic requirements by turning out "correct" material in the form of Brahmsian exercises, proving that he could write "pretty" music when he had to.

After graduating from Yale, young Ives was faced with an important decision. He had prepared himself thoroughly for a career in music, but he was realistic enough to realize that the kind of music he wanted to write would not readily find a public. Since he was not about to write any other kind, he knew that he would undoubtedly face a rough road should he follow his own inspiration.

Rather than compromise his art, Ives decided to make himself financially independent of music. He entered the business world and specialized in insurance. After working in the field for several years, he organized the firm of Ives & Merrick in 1909. The firm prospered under his management and Ives remained with the firm until ill health forced his retirement in 1930.

Music, then, became an avocation for one of the most original minds in all of music. Despite the fact that he was never able to devote all of his time to composition, Ives managed to complete an impressive body of work which includes four major symphonies and the uncompleted portion of a fifth, violin and piano sonatas, numerous orchestral sketches and tone poems, two string quartets, literally hundreds of songs, and a number of substantial choral works.

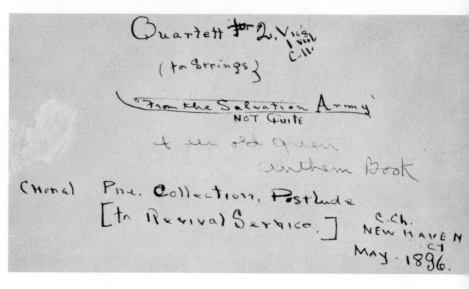

The title page of Ives's first quartet with a characteristically irreverent epigraph.

Revealed in this body of work is a composer of startling originality and inventiveness whose music is intimately related to the American scene. This interest is indicated in the titles: "Thanksgiving" (1904); "Washington's Birthday" (1909); "Decoration Day" (1912); "Fourth of July" (1913); and "Three Places in New England" (1903–1914). What is probably his best known work, the Second Piano Sonata (1909–1915), is subtitled "Concord, Mass., 1840–60" and its four movements are named after the writers, Emerson, Hawthorne, the Alcotts, and Thoreau.

His raw material for all of this work was the ordinary musical life of a small New England town. In his search for musical vigor and vitality Ives accepted all music. An ordinary hymn tune, for him, was as inspiring as a symphony; a circus band as valid a musical vehicle as a chamber orchestra. He borrowed generously from the traditions and styles of European art music and fused it with American popular and folk traditions.

In evolving his highly individualistic musical language, Ives used popular dance hall tunes, fragments of hymns and patriotic anthems, brass band marches, country dances, and songs which he integrated into works of enormous complexity. He freely used multiple cross-rhythms, sharp dissonances, tone-clusters, polytonality, wide melodic skips, jazz effects, assymetrical rhythmic patterns, quarter-tone effects, and he employed all of these advanced techniques with verve and rare humor. It must also be remembered that all of these techniques were new when he employed them, though many were later incorporated into the language of modern music. He arrived at these procedures independently, for many of his innovations preceded their use by the *avant-garde* composers of Europe. Charles Ives will go down in history as one of the most inventive composers of modern times.

As we can well imagine, Ives's music was hardly popular with the broad public at the time it was written. The composer found it all but impossible to get his music performed and as a result became something of a musical recluse. Occasionally he would lash out at the "nice, lily-eared" public, as he did when he attended a performance of an atonal work by another composer in Boston. The work was booed by the audience and Ives, irked by this response, stood up from his chair and shouted at the audience, calling the people there "cowards, afraid to listen to tough music like men . . . afraid they might hurt their nice ears."

This attitude, tempered by an irrepressible humor, spills over into many of Ives's scores in rather color-ful directional notations. In a particularly raucous passage he may ask the performer to "knock them in the aisle," or "roar until their ears hurt." In his Second String Quartet, Ives calls the second violin Rollo, for whom he writes sweetly sentimental pas-sages marked "pretty tune for the ladies, Rollo." When the music grows fast and furious, blackening the page with notes and accidentals, Ives adds in the margin: "Too hard to play—*so it just can't be good music,* Rollo." Finally, he asks Rollo to "Join in again, Professor, all in the key of C. You can do that nice and pretty."

On another occasion Ives remarked discouragingly upon the response to his music of a celebrated violinist:

> Well, the "professor" came, and after a lot of big talk he started to play the first movement of the First Sonata. He didn't even get through the first page. . . . "This cannot be played," he said. . . . "this is awful . . . this is not music!" . . . After he had left, I had a kind of feeling which I have had on and off when other celebrated musicians have seen, or played, or tried to play my music. Said I to myself, "Am I the only one who likes any of my music. . . . No one else seems to hear it the same way. Are MY EARS ON WRONG?"

In his notes to the second piano sonata, the *Concord Sonata,* Ives answers critics who complained about the apparent formlessness of the music:

> ... and when the nice old ladies say "no design ...
> formless ... all music should have design & form."
> "Yes, Sarah, but not necessarily your design and
> form ... no siree!"

Today the music of Charles Ives is a little less challenging to the public ear. We have become somewhat accustomed to atonality and dissonance. It is a measure of the revolutionary character of Ives that his music still sounds as daring and contemporary as it does. Had this music been performed at the time it was written it would most certainly have had the same kind of impact that the works of Schoenberg, Berg, and Stravinsky had in Europe. But the music of Ives was too far in advance of the mainstream of American

In his Second String Quartet, Ives jibes at the second violin,
"Too hard to play—so it just can't be good music, Rollo."

music. When his compositions were finally performed with a degree of acceptance and regularity, Ives was already an old man and many of his daring innovations appeared "old hat."

Ives's Second Symphony, for example, which he worked on between 1897 and 1902, received its first performance in 1951 when it was played by the Philharmonic-Symphony Orchestra of New York, under Leonard Bernstein. His Third Symphony, completed in 1911, was first performed in 1945. The Fourth Symphony, written between 1910 and 1916, received its première in 1965 under the direction of Leopold Stokowski. Not until he was awarded the Pulitzer Prize for his Third Symphony, in 1947, did Charles Ives receive any degree of recognition for his work.

Working alone, for the most part, without public recognition or performance, Ives embraced within his compositions America's musical past, present, and future. Nearly all of his works were written before 1920. Then, suffering from chronic diabetes and hand tremor, and discouraged by the almost universal neglect of his music, he gave up composition. Charles Ives died in New York City on May 19, 1954.

Fortunately, he lived long enough to enjoy a somewhat belated recognition. He not only heard his own music being performed in the concert halls, but also saw a confirmation of his musical ideas which had generated so much hostility when they were written. He also saw America's composers turning to a native musical tradition for their inspiration and form—a tradition that Ives had loved and respected long before the academy recognized its validity for American music.

12. AMERICAN MUSIC TODAY

AMERICA, more than any other country, is a polyglot nation. Its population derives from people all over the world and its cultural traditions reflect this background. American music, as we have seen, is made up of many different national strains and traditions. Over the years this musical patchwork quilt has fused into a language and syntax that is distinctively American. It took some three hundred years for this amalgamation to occur and even more time before its validity and authenticity could be appreciated.

The twentieth century has been a period of consolidation and fruition. The most significant feature of this period has been the merging and resolution of two conflicting views of the nature of music and art. The genteel tradition of the nineteenth century split American music into two conflicting poles. It isolated art music in an ivory tower that ignored an authentic body of folk and popular music that evolved in response to the peculiar conditions of the New World outside the academy.

Although the genteel tradition spawned a steady stream of composers throughout the nineteenth century, they produced little of lasting musical value. Dominated by the art music of Europe, they failed to recognize the undeniable musical genius taking shape at home. What this tradition did contribute to American music was the establishment of a precedent of professional competence in both performance and composition. When the genteel tradition was finally absorbed into the mainstream of the popular and folk expression that flourished outside the academy, American music, to an important degree, came of age.

This maturity is reflected in the state of American music today. One of the most interesting characteristics of twentieth-century music in the United States has been the absorption of popular and commercial forms into the realm of art. We have seen, for example, the dramatic development of jazz. Spawned in the saloons and honky-tonks of New Orleans, jazz has evolved within a time span of no more than fifty years into a supple, improvisational music form that has won a respected place in the concert halls of the world.

Equally dramatic has been the rise of musical comedy which has been transformed from a bawdy, vulgar music hall entertainment into a new, indigenous art form. American musical comedy has developed its own peculiar styles, theatrical presence, and lyric language. Most serious musicologists today will agree on the significance of this lyric form in the musical life of the twentieth century.

In the history of musical comedy we can trace an interesting parallel to the growth of American art music. Musical comedy, as it has evolved in the professional theatre, represents a synthesis, a coming together, of two traditions: the vulgar, bawdy, exuberant minstrel show, burlesque, and vaudeville; and the Viennese, French, and German schools of light opera and operetta.

At the beginning of the twentieth century these two traditions were mutually exclusive. The American lyric theatre was dominated on the one hand by such European trained and inspired composers as Victor Herbert, Sigmund Romberg and Franz Lehar; on the other by a homegrown mélange of vaudeville, burlesque, and minstrel. Then, beginning in the second decade of this century, a number of composers combined these two musical forms into a radically new kind of lyric theatre.

This transformation began with the work of George M. Cohan and Irving Berlin. Their productions incorporated elements of popular expression such as ragtime and jazz into a theatrical form that took the lyric theatre out of imaginary Balkan principalities into the real world. Dramatic advances in the technical aspects of staging and lighting during this period further tended to raise the artistic level of musical comedy.

During this same period the "intimate" comedies of Jerome Kern introduced believable plot construction and characterization. Then, in the early thirties, political satire was added. *Of Thee I Sing*, by George Gershwin, typified this kind of topical, hard-hitting entertainment which made musical comedy still more realistic and believable.

In the late 1930's and early 1940's, a stylized ballet was introduced into musical comedy. Such outstanding choreographers as George Ballanchine, Agnes DeMille, and Michael Kidd established the dance as an integrated element in the storytelling of the musical comedy form. The entire emphasis in performance changed subtly. Music and story line became the dominant factor—at the expense of the individual star who dominated earlier musical comedy—and, for the first time, musical comedy became based upon the combined efforts of score, scenery, ballet, costumes, music, and story, all of which moved in an integrated lyric form.

The culmination was the brilliant series of musical comedies composed by Richard Rodgers together with the lyricists Lorenz Hart and, later, Oscar Hammerstein II. *Oklahoma!* (1943), by Rodgers and Hammerstein, provides one of the important high points in this development. One of the most successful musical comedies of all times, it provided a prototype for subsequent efforts in this form. Here was a completely American musical comedy, different in character and idiom from anything known in Europe, different even from what had been standard Broadway fare.

As produced on the stage, *Oklahoma!* is a completely integrated theatrical experience. All of its elements— music, lyrics, choreography, songs, settings, story line,

American musical comedy is different in character and idiom from anything known in Europe. Above, the Ascot Gavotte from the successful show My Fair Lady.

characterizations—serve to advance the action and enhance the telling of a story in terms of music and dance. With *Oklahoma!* American musical comedy created a distinctive national character.

The vitality of this home-grown form has been demonstrated by the later history of the Amerian lyric theatre. This tradition has been carried further by such outstanding composers as Leonard Bernstein (*West Side Story, Candide*); George Abbot and Bob Merrill (*New Girl In Town*); Frank Loesser (*Most Happy Fella*), and Allan Jay Lerner and Frederick Loewe (*My Fair Lady*).

171

In the area of popular music mid-twentieth-century America has again demonstrated the ability to produce a music to which the people of the world can respond. Rock and roll is the music of this period and its popularity has swept the world. In one respect the popularity of this form represents a musical regression. It takes its drive and impetus from the earliest, most primitive forms of country music and gospel singing. In another respect rock and roll has been a potent and liberating force in popular music.

In its wake all the clichés of the older ballad, jazz, and swing styles, both instrumental and vocal, have been swept away. Because it breaks so radically with tradition, rock and roll has generated an entire language of new performance techniques. It exploits the voice, for example, in completely novel and unexpected ways, raising the glissando, speech, and falsetto to new levels of expressiveness. Instrumental sounds, in this genre, have evolved completely unorthodox patterns while the unabashed utilization of electronic techniques has radically upset the old instrumental balances. Harmonic development in rock and roll becomes directly allied with the straightforward, driving rhythm, and exploits tonal combinations that were studiously avoided in the past.

The result is a combination of the earthiness and vigor of the earliest jazz styles with the advanced techniques of modern electronics, in a driving, pulsating, musical style that has captured the imagination of the world. The extent of this dominance is revealed in the casual street-corner singing of today's teenagers. Only ten years ago this kind of singing was characterized by harmonization based upon the common triad. Today anything goes, and one hears the most outlandish combination of tones that range from parallel fifths to the most complex kind of diminished-seventh chords—sounds that would have been dismissed as the worst kinds of dissonance only yesterday.

In the more formal area of fine art music, America has emerged in this second half of the twentieth century as a leading contributor. Literally dozens of American composers in this vein have gained international status and their combined efforts are capable of holding their own with most of the contemporary music being composed anywhere. Today America supports a thriving musical establishment with hundreds of symphony orchestras—many of them first rate—fine schools and conservatories and an appreciative audience.

Probably the most significant evidence of the vitality of American music is demonstrated in our relationship to our most radical and experimental composers. Even so controversial a figure as John Cage can attract respectable audiences and earn a livelihood through the composition of works that push at the very limits of music as it is familiarly understood.

Actually, twentieth-century American music has been characterized by this kind of radical experimenting. Charles Ives, as we have already seen, stretched the traditional limits of musical expressions into areas that have subsequently been incorporated into the standard language of contemporary music. In the twenties, George Antheil scandalized his contemporaries with his *Ballet Mécanique* and *Jazz Symphony*. A little later Henry Dixon Cowell experimented with "tone-clusters" in both piano and orchestral works. He also invented an instrument called the "Rhythmicon" which was designed to reproduce, with complete mechanical accuracy, all kinds of rhythms and metrical patterns. The instrument was first demonstrated in New York in January 1932, at the New School for Social Research in a four-movement suite, titled *Rhythmicana,* for orchestra and Rhythmicon.

Harry Partch, a self-taught composer who spent much of his early life in remote areas of the Arizona and New Mexico deserts, has evolved a completely individual musical vocabulary exploited by a number of instruments he invented himself. Partch's music is based upon a forty-three-tone octave system that gives coherence to his monophonically conceived approach to sound. Partch, singlehandedly, has attempted to bring music back to its prehistoric origins using shouts, whines, grunts, and repetitive chants in an exploration of the human subconscious which gave birth to all music.

Probably the most influential of our experimentalist composers is the previously mentioned John Cage. Cage was born in Los Angeles, California, in 1912, and by the time he was twenty he was already exploring unusual sonorities and tonal combinations of the piano. He studied composition and harmony with Henry Cowell, Adolph Weiss, and Arnold Schoenberg.

Nearly all of Cage's earliest music was composed either for percussion or "prepared" piano—an ordinary piano whose strings have been muted with an assortment of miscellaneous small objects, such as bits of wood, rubber, metal, glass, bolts, screws, rubber bands, weather-stripping, etc. The specific type of "preparation" changes for each composition while an occasional "unprepared" tone is also permitted. In these works Cage's sonorous effects are characterized by a delicate, carefully controlled and calculated execution. At best his prepared piano pieces project a sound that is reminiscent of the Javanese gamelon with its wooden chimes, bronze slabs, bamboo pipes, and metal disks that blend into a miniature, enchanting, aural experience.

Since then Cage has extended his experimentation to include random sound, silence, and electronics. One of his compositions is scored for twelve radios, twenty-four performers, and conductor. Two performers are stationed at each radio. One manipulates the dynamics while the other switches stations. The wave lengths (stations) to be tuned in at any given moment are indicated on the score, along with dynamic instructions. Since the radio content will change at different times and in different areas, the actual sound produced is random and completely accidental.

Cage has also investigated the electronic tape as a source of "musical" experimentation. In "Williams Mix," for example, he seems to have deliberately selected and processed the most grotesque noises available. The sound, recorded on magnetic tape and reproduced according to specific notations, consists of city noises, country sounds, pure electronic whines, manually produced sounds, wind-produced sounds, and small sounds—dripping water, breathing, etc.—greatly amplified. The frequency, duration, pitch, and dynamics of the "mix" are controlled by chance operations.

The remarkable thing about Cage is the fact that so eccentric and challenging a composer is not an isolated figure. On the contrary, Cage has earned the status of an *avant-garde* saint whose disciples proliferate steadily. His concerts are well attended, if not well received, by many, and his lectures are popular wherever he appears.

Another interesting development in American music today is the continuing exploration of the use of electronically produced music. The theremin, vibraphone, and other electronic instruments which have been freely exploited, especially in the musical scores for films, are fairly familiar instruments. Less known, perhaps, are the new, highly complex, musical "synthesizers." The RCA music synthesizer, for example, operates from a coded tape, punched with all the fundamental factors required to form a musical sound—pitch, duration, loudness, rate of attack, rate of decay, reverberation, harmonics, vibrato, and electrical "noise." Theoretically, this electronic maze can reproduce any sound known and can generate new sounds that have never before occurred.

The potentiality of electronic music is only beginning to be explored. Today many composers are working with these instruments, and the range and extent of their possibilities remain one of the most exciting developments in contemporary music.

Thus American music has progressed from the metrical psalm tunes of the Pilgrims to the random accidental sounds of a John Cage "symphony"; from a complex African percussive tradition to the esoteric glissandos of "third stream" jazz. In the interim America has evolved a distinct national voice whose echo is heard today in all the music of the world. Yet this is

The RCA music synthesizer has a capacity of originating endless varieties of rhythms. It brings together familiar sounds and creates an unlimited range of tone variations.

only a beginning. America appears to be in the midst of what can be best described as a cultural renaissance. Our bold experimenters are exploring new areas of expression in all the arts. American painters and sculptors have startled the world with the originality and power of their vision, just as our poets and writers have sought out new forms to express a new culture that has proliferated throughout the entire world. In many respects, however, American music remains the most vital area of our artistic life, and music may well prove to be our most significant contribution to the twentieth century—the one thing above all others that we may be best remembered for in the future.

Bibliography

Aptheker, Herbert (ed.), *A Documentary History of the Negro People in the United States.* New York, The Citadel Press, 1951.

Armstrong, Louis, *Swing That Music.* London, Longmans, Green and Co., Ltd., 1936.

Bauer, Marion, *Twentieth Century Music.* New York, G. P. Putnam's Sons, 1933.

Blesh, Rudi and Harriet Janis, *They All Played Ragtime: The True Story of an American Music.* New York, Alfred A. Knopf, Inc., 1950.

Chase, Gilbert, *America's Music.* New York, McGraw-Hill Book Company, Inc., 1955.

Copland, Aaron, *Our New Music: Leading Composers in Europe and America.* New York, McGraw-Hill Book Company, Inc., 1941.

Cowell, Henry (ed.), *American Composers on American Music.* Stanford, Calif., Stanford University Press, 1933.

Cowell, Henry and Sidney, *Charles Ives and His Music.* New York, Oxford University Press, Inc., 1954.

DuBois, William E. B., *Black Folk: Then and Now.* New York, Henry Holt & Company, 1939.

Eaton, Quaintance, *Musical U.S.A.* New York, Allan, Towne & Heathe, Inc., 1949.

Finkelstein, Sidney, *Jazz: A People's Music.* New York, The Citadel Press, 1948.

Handy, W. C., *Father of the Blues: An Autobiography.* New York, The Macmillan Company, 1940.

Howard, John Tasker, *Our American Music: Three Hundred Years of It,* New York, Thomas Y. Crowell Company, 1946.

Levant, Oscar, *A Smattering of Ignorance.* New York, Doubleday, Doran and Company, 1940.

Mason, Daniel Gregory, *Music in My Time.* New York, The Macmillan Company, 1938.

Mellers, Wilfred, *Music in a New Found Land.* New York, Alfred A. Knopf, Inc., 1964.

Partch, Harry, *Genesis of a Music.* Madison, Wisconsin, The University of Wisconsin Press, 1949.

Phillips, Ulrich B., *Life and Labor in the Old South.* Boston, Little, Brown and Company, 1929.

Rice, Edward Leroy, *Monarchs of Minstrelsy.* New York, Kenny Publishing Company, 1911.

Ritter, Frederic Louis, *Music in America.* New York, Charles Scribner's Sons, 1883.

Sewall, Samuel, *Diary,* Mark Van Doren, ed. New York, Macy-Masius, 1927.

Spaeth, Sigmund, *A History of Popular Music in America.* New York, Random House, Inc., 1948.

Sweet, William Warren, *The Story of Religion in America.* New York, Harper & Brothers, 1950.

INDEX

Abbott, George, 171
Accomplished Synger (Mather), 21–22
Adagio for harmonica solo, (Mozart), 42
Ainsworth, Henry, 16
Ainsworth Psalter, 13, 16–17
Alcott family, 162
American In Paris, An (Gershwin), 152
Antheil, George, 173–174
Armstrong, Louis, 131, 135, 137, 138
"As I Walked Down the Streets of Laredo," 80

Bach, Johann Christian, 24
Bach, Johann Sebastian, 104, 105, 157
Bach, Karl Philipp Emanuel, 24, 43
Baker, Theodore, 54
"Ballad Creole" (Gottschalk), 121
Ballanchine, George, 170
Ballet Mécanique (Antheil), 174
"Bananier, Le" (Gottschalk), 121
"Bamboula, La" (Gottschalk), 121
"Barbara Allen," 77–78
Barber, Samuel, 9
Barnum, P. T., 122
Bay Psalm Book, 17
"Beautiful Dreamer, Wake unto Me," 96
Bechet, Sidney, 7, 132
Beethoven, Ludwig von, 2–3, 42, 43, 45, 104, 157
Beissel, Johann Conrad, 27-31, 37
Berg, Alban, 165
Berlin, Irving, 68, 169
Berlioz, Hector, 121–122
Bernstein, Leonard, 9, 166, 171
Blake, William, 33
Boccherini, Luigi, 43
Bolden, Charles "Buddy," 7, 130–131

Botetourt, Baron, 67
Bower, Frank, 87
Brahms, Johannes, 104, 157, 161
Brewster, William, 13
Bridges, Josiah, 36
Briggs, London, 67
Bristow, George Frederick, 102–103
Browne, Edmund, 14
Brusle, Aimée Marie de, 120
Bryant, Dan, 5
Bryant's Minstrels, 93
Buck, Dudley, 105, 106, 108
Burleigh, Henry Thacker, 117

Cadman, Charles Wakefield, 56
Cage, John, 173–177
"Camptown Races" (Foster), 94
"Canada Iho," 80
"Canal Street Blues," 137
Candide (Bernstein), 171
Cantata to the American Flag (Dvořák), 116
Carter, Robert, 40
Chadwick, George, 108
"Chanson Negre" (Gottschalk), 121
Chopin, Frédéric François, 121, 122
Christy, Edwin P., 87, 94 95
Christy Minstrels, The, 87–89
Civil War, 58, 87, 93, 127–129
Coates, Albert, 151
Cohan, George M., 169
Coleman, Ornette, 143–144
"Collegium Musicum," 23–24, 26
Columbus (Bristow), 103
Community of the Solitary, 27, 29, 37
Concerto in F (Gershwin), 151–152
Concord Sonata (Ives), 162, 164–165
Condon, Eddie, 139
Copland, Aaron, 9
Corelli, Arcangelo, 43
Cotton, John, 14, 16

181

INDEX 🐚

184